Attention-Deficit/
Hyperactivity Disorder
in the Classroom

D1613559

Attention-Deficit/ Hyperactivity Disorder in the Classroom

A Practical Guide for Teachers

Carol A. Dowdy
James R. Patton
Tom E. C. Smith
Edward A. Polloway

pro·ed
8700 Shoal Creek Boulevard
Austin, Texas 78757-6897

pro·ed

© 1998 by PRO-ED, Inc.
8700 Shoal Creek Boulevard
Austin, Texas 78757-6897

Library of Congress Cataloging-in-Publication Data

Attention-Deficit/Hyperactivity disorder in the classroom: a
    practical guide for teachers / Carol A. Dowdy . . . [et al.].
        p.   cm.
    Includes bibliographical references and index.
    ISBN (invalid) 0-89079-665-3 (pbk. : alk. paper)
    1. Attention-deficit-disordered children—Education—United
States.   2. Attention-deficit hyperactivity disorder—United States.
    I. Dowdy, Carol Ammons.
LC4713.4.A89   1997
371.93—dc21   96-39435
                                                             CIP

This book is designed in Eras and Palatino.

Production Manager: Alan Grimes
Production Coordinator: Karen Swain
Managing Editor: Tracy Sergo
Designer: Thomas Barkley
Reprints Buyer: Alicia Woods
Editor: Jill Mason
Production Assistant: Claudette Landry
Editorial Assistant: Suzi Hunn

Printed in the United States of America

1 2 3 4 5 6 7 8 9 10   01 00 99 98

Contents

Preface

This book came to be as a result of an awareness that teachers wanted more information on how to meet the needs of students in their classes who were being referred to as attention-deficit disordered (ADD) or attention-deficit/hyperactivity disordered (ADHD). (We will use the latter term throughout this book, as it is the umbrella term designated by the American Psychiatric Association.) The concerns of these teachers were real. They felt unprepared to deal with this group of students, who were mostly found in general education. Few, if any, opportunities occurred in their training programs to address this issue. For that matter, few textbooks written for introductory courses in exceptionality include material on attention-deficit/hyperactivity disorder. Inservice training has not typically provided the practical ideas that are needed.

This book is not exhaustive, yet it contains the major topics that will be helpful to teachers. It also contains information found nowhere else. For instance, few resources have addressed the issue of transition from school age to young adulthood very well. This book dedicates an entire chapter to that issue.

Like a worldwide web site with links to other sites, this book links the reader to other resources that might be helpful if more detailed information is needed. Yet most of the topics here are presented in a way that leads directly to instructional practice and implementation.

The thinking of the authors of this book has evolved over time on the issue of how best to serve this population of students. Early on, we felt that this group was being adequately served under existing categorical distinctions in the Individuals with Disabilities Act (IDEA).

However, after much contact with families of students who had been identified as ADHD but whose needs were not being met in school, we realized that those families were living with great frustration—they were told that their children had problems, yet those problems were not being addressed.

To assist families in dealing with the realities of ADHD, a number of actions are warranted. One of them is to provide the teachers of their children with resources to better understand and serve those students. We hope that this book is such a resource. We have strived to develop a book that is easy to use and filled with practical suggestions in the major areas associated with school activities.

Because ADHD is a condition that affects many different people, we decided to start the book off with a personal account. We want to thank Maureen Neuville for sharing her and her family's experiences with us. A more extensive treatise on Maureen's experiences, *Sometimes I Get All Scribbly: Living with Attention-Deficit/Hyperactivity Disorder*, is also available from PRO-ED. It is a mother's testament to the day-to-day, moment-by-moment existence of life with a child who is hyperactive. It validates the struggles and triumphs of their lives.

We are also grateful to others for their assistance with the development of this book. As all authors know, no book would ever see a printing press without the hard work of many people. We are grateful to Kathy Fad for her contribution on school-based collaboration. Once again, we thank Gwenn Long for her clerical assistance. The production staff at PRO-ED were great. We are very appreciative of the efforts of Alan Grimes and Tracy Sergo for their support during the production phase. The cover design, which we like very much, is the work of Lee Anne Landry. The way the book is written was improved substantially because of the work of our copyeditor, Jill Mason.

We are hopeful that something within the covers of this book has an impact on the students for whom this book was written.

CHAPTER 1

Case Study: Brian[1]

Maureen Bissen Neuville

Brian's birth could only be described as "fast and furious." As an infant, Brian slept little. He was awake to be fed every 2 to 2½ hours for weeks and didn't sleep all night even once until he was six months old. He gave up naps when he was barely two and still awoke by 6:00 A.M.

Despite his early awakenings, through his second year Brian was often content to sit in one spot with a single activity for quite a while. He did not creep or crawl much and did not walk until nearly sixteen months old. He was especially fond of toys with many small parts and would play with them endlessly. Often his play consisted of throwing books, emptying drawers, or disassembling toys, though he had neither the desire nor the ability to reconstruct even the simplest ones.

By age two, Brian's behavior began to worry Mark and me. He still awoke early and would come bounding into our bedroom and climb in bed, not *with* us but on *top* of us. He would wiggle and bounce and do his best to annoy us. He loved to put his fingers and feet in our faces, not to mention his smelly, diapered bottom!

---

[1]The purpose of including a case study early in the book is to provide the reader with a personal feel for attention-deficit/hyperactive disorder. Because much of the book is intended to share classroom-related information in the form of suggestions and practices to address the educational needs of students with ADHD, we believe it is important to always be aware of the individual who is striving to deal with the demands of school. Brian's story is related by his mother, who has written a more in-depth work, *Sometimes I Get All Scribbly: Living with Attention-Deficit/Hyperactivity Disorder* (1995), about her family's struggles to deal with ADHD. We think that this personal account sets the tone and establishes the need for the chapters that follow.

It took a great deal of physical and emotional energy to keep up with Brian—he was persistent and demanded much attention. His brother was nearly four years older, and the two rarely played together. When they did interact, it was with tussles and shouts; we were constantly pulling them apart. Brian was often whiny, aggressive, and uncooperative. He seemed never to comply with our requests and loudly resisted our commands. Neither discipline nor rewards could entice him to change his actions. "Boys will be boys," others said. But I wondered, and worried what might be wrong with our son. Some days he scared me, the way he seemed driven to extremes.

We talked to our pediatrician, who reminded us about time-outs and discipline and gave us a book on parenting techniques. We also attended some classes on positive parenting. We were already doing most of what the book and the class suggested, but nothing seemed to work, not for long anyway. We hoped it was just a stage.

Over the next two years, Brian exhibited some disturbing behaviors, including bouncing into walls and wiggling his fingers in other people's faces. And he was always asking others to "shut up," even if they were speaking in the next room. He seemed as annoyed and frustrated with others as we were with him.

Mark and I received an abundance of advice. Some thought we were too harsh on him. Others said to give him a good spanking (though we'd done that; it only made his behavior worse). We were absorbed in frustration and worry about Brian's actions and wondered if we were to blame.

His frequent, almost constant, wiggle-jiggle, poke, and prod made it difficult for anyone to be around him. We were becoming desperate; Brian's conduct and our reactions to it were not doing good things for our family life. Holidays were a disaster; going to church was hell.

Even at age four, Brian made few attempts to color or draw and would not try to use a scissors. We were eager to have him tested in our school district's routine preschool screening to see if a reason could be found for his struggles. I also hoped his speech could be improved, since most people had a hard time understanding him. When the testing was done, he showed poor motor-skill control. A few of his attempts at copying shapes are reproduced on the next page.

He scored within the normal range on most test sections, however, and the school personnel felt that his articulation skills would catch up by the time he was in kindergarten. He was not accepted into the preschool program for children with disabilities, since there were

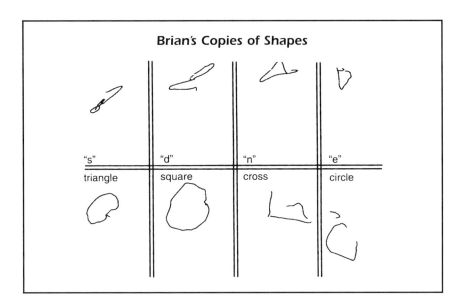

Brian's Copies of Shapes

| "s" | "d" | "n" | "e" |
| triangle | square | cross | circle |

others of greater apparent need. We were disappointed, but instead we enrolled him in a private preschool.

In preschool, Brian surprised us by acting shy and withdrawn. For the first few weeks, he would retreat from the group and lie flat on the floor, rocking gently and looking around. As the year progressed, he assumed the role of onlooker instead of participant in group activities. His teacher told us in a kind but puzzled way, "I've never met a child like Brian." She also questioned whether Brian could hear properly, since he often seemed not to respond to her requests. We, too, were having difficulty with compliance at home. We had his hearing professionally checked; it was fine.

Then our third son was born. Brian was becoming increasingly aggressive and noncompliant. He was still up early, and his baby brother woke twice during the night. Mark and I were exhausted and were experiencing much strain on our marriage and our interactions with the children.

And yet Brian could also be delightful, especially when I was with him alone. I tried to appreciate his positive qualities; in fact, I often called him my "sweetie boy." But he was so intense! Even when he hugged, it was too long and too hard, until we had to pry him away.

Brian had a way of expressing himself that was unique and perceptive beyond his years. When we would give him directions for a task, he would shake his head and say, "I get all scribbly." He rarely completed even a simple task without several reminders. He could hardly pick up a pair of socks and put them both on without being distracted or wandering off. This pervasive inattentive behavior is almost more disruptive to family functioning than the more blatant misbehaviors. He also expressed confusion over his actions when he told me, "I have two sides to my brain, one that makes me be good and one that makes me be bad."

When Brian had just turned five, my sister visited; she taught school in a distant state. She asked if we had heard of attention-deficit/hyperactivity disorder (ADHD). We had not, but we were willing to check it out.

We talked to our pediatrician, who said that Brian might or might not have ADHD. She explained that children with ADHD benefited from medication. Mark and I would not take what we saw as the easy way out; we refused to medicate our child, and so we struggled on.

We tried to remain positive, but Brian's aggression and noncompliance made it difficult for us to avoid constantly reprimanding him. He was very emotional and cried much more than the average five year old.

So this is the child we took to school; we explained our concerns to his kindergarten teacher and hoped she could help. Kindergarten brought social conflicts due to Brian's excessive activity level and inability to stick with a task. An evaluation by school personnel determined that he did not have specific learning disabilities, but he was enrolled in speech therapy and a "friendship" social skills group.

Meanwhile at home, Mark and I tried to maintain consistency and a positive attitude with our three busy boys, now ages nine, five, and one. But we could not leave Brian alone with either of his brothers for even a few minutes, so he had to stay by our side at all times. We put locks on the bathroom doors, not to keep others out but to keep Brian in with us. He would have to make several trips with me from the house to the car and back each day as I loaded the baby into his carseat and got him and his older brother out the door to school. Babysitters were hard to find for our three active boys, and some who came were unwilling to come back.

By now, Mark and I were desperate and agreed that medication might be necessary. We met with a clinical child psychologist, who conducted a thorough evaluation. I began to read about ADHD, and the more I read, the more it sounded like Brian. When he was diagnosed with the disorder, we felt relieved. We now knew what we were dealing with and had a direction in helping Brian with his troubles.

Brian has always been very aware of what is difficult for him—curbing his impulses, following directions, for example. With our newfound knowledge, Mark and I now educated him about the disorder that caused those difficulties. He met other children his age with the same disorder. Mark and I became active in a support group for parents called CHADD (Children with ADD). Through this group, we learned even more and were able to advocate in our community for everyone with the disorder.

Brian was put on a trial of methylphenidate (Ritalin). At first, we gave him medication only during school hours, and he showed almost immediate improvement. But evenings and weekends continued to be riddled with strife, so we began to give it to him at home as well. With the medication, he had better control of his impulses and responded more positively to our behavior modification plans and charts that had been so ineffective before. The quality of life was much better for all of us. Others noticed Brian's improvement and commented on it as well. Mark and I continued to work regularly with Brian's psychologist; our ongoing contact with her has proven to be a crucial part of his multimodal treatment.

Unfortunately, Brian continued to have difficulties at school because his behavior was still significantly different from that of his peers. Throughout first grade he acted impulsively, and classmates noticed and shunned him. He wandered in a sea of loneliness on the playground. He also experienced petit mal seizures and migraine headaches. He was easily annoyed by sounds and very tactilely sensitive. None of his conditions were severe, but with him struggling in so many areas, I often looked at him with a heavy heart.

He had no friends and almost no interactions with other children outside of school. We offered to arrange opportunities and encouraged him to meet with classmates, but he either acted indifferent or resisted. Throughout the rest of elementary school, he remained socially inept. He experienced short periods of friendship with two classmates but did not have the skills to sustain them. Though I was disappointed when these acquaintances stopped contacting him, Brian seemed almost relieved; he was more comfortable alone than having to deal with other people. Even so, he did feel left out and often expressed his loneliness, such as the time he told me, "I'm just a waste of skin."

In the second grade, we started using a weekly goal card system. After goals for appropriate school behaviors had been established, Brian's teacher would rate his behavior daily as poor, better, or good. Points were given, and for reaching a targeted number of points for the week, Brian received a reward. This system had three distinct advantages: it gave Brian a way to monitor his behaviors; it reinforced him for appropriate actions; and it was an efficient way of communicating daily between teachers and home. We continued the goal cards through the fifth grade. Here is a reproduction of one of his goal cards:

Example of Brian's Goal Card

GOAL CARD PROGRAM (I)ntermediate
Grades One - Eight

Child's Name _Brian Neuville_   Teacher _Mr. G._

Grade _4_   School _____   Home Room _____

Week of _Oct. 14-18_   * Brian had university student helping him

Goal Card	MON	TUE	WED	THU	FRI	Rating Scales
Paid attention in class	2	2	2	2		N/A = Not Applicable
Completed work in class	3	3	2	3		O = Losing, Forgetting or Destroying Card
Completed homework	3	2	2	2		CHECK SCALE TO BE USED
Wrote down assignments	3	2.5	2.5	3		1 = Poor
Extras to remember	2	1	2	2		2 = Better / 3 = Good
Total	13	10½	10½	12		Wed – practice handwriting write more in journal
Teacher's Initials	JG	JG	JG	JG		Try For _42_ Points
Parents initials	MN	MN	MN	MN		Mon. night / Didn't bring home folder

When I requested use of the goal card, some teachers were reluctant, assuming it would take too much time. I would counter with, "Will you try it for two weeks?" to which they could hardly say no. And after that, every one found that it took only seconds at the end of the day and kept Brian very much on task and working hard for his weekly goal treats.

I always approached Brian's classroom teachers—including "specials" like music and art—just before the beginning of a school year. I gave each a small packet of information on ADHD and highlighted the areas that Brian had special difficulty with, plus mentioning his assets. I asked for special seating placement, frequent contact from the school staff, and tolerance of his idiosyncrasies as long as they were not disrupting others or breaking school rules. I also made sure that other school personnel—secretary, cook, and aides—were aware of his disorder. It was only fair to them as well as to my son that they knew that Brian had special needs and that I wanted to know if he was being disruptive or seemed to be struggling.

While home life was going better, we were still under the strain of managing Brian in the early mornings before medication and evenings after the medication wore off. This was complicated by the demands of two other children, one of whom was entering the terrible twos.

We continued to use behavior modification charts and other techniques at home, at the suggestion of and with constant encouragement from Brian's psychologist. It was hard to be patient and consistent, but we usually succeeded, though not always! There were times when Mark or I would become so frustrated and angry, we would have to leave the room, or even the house, until we could handle ourselves properly again. Behaviors of children with ADHD elicit an array of emotions within those that care for them.

By fourth grade, Brian had improved enough that he was no longer being ridiculed by his classmates—nor was he accepted by them; they simply tolerated him. Despite our work and encouragement, he still had few positive social skills. His lack of friends, or even any social contact, continued to hang heavy on my heart.

Little things that teachers have done have meant so much to us. His fourth-grade teacher thought of using an in-class cue to keep Brian alert and on task. The teacher made a deal with Brian that whenever he rested his hand on Brian's desk it meant either that something important was being said, or that Brian had been obviously daydreaming. Brian's desk was in the front row, and the teacher could easily lean forward while talking and give the cue in a casual and natural manner. The teacher also made sure to touch the desks of other front-row children; no one else ever knew what was going on between Brian and him.

Brian continued to be aware of his struggles and also of his new-found successes. We complimented him at home whenever we could. He told us once, referring to his earlier years, "I'm not like that anymore." (True, but he still had a long way to go.)

During fifth grade Brian blossomed. He was in a new school, and instead of being intimidated by that, he seemed to think it would be a fresh start; these children had not known that "old Brian." His teacher was a godsend—he expected much of his students but in an encouraging way.

This teacher recognized Brian's talent in math and allowed him to work ahead individually into the sixth-grade book; this was a big boost for Brian's self-esteem. While he was doing well in the classroom, however, he was struggling with the load of homework. It was difficult to get him to organize his papers and remember to bring materials home. He had an assignment notebook, but he didn't always write them down. Or if he did, he would be confused by evening as to what the teacher had asked them to do. Instead of behavioral tasks on Brian's goal card, we now switched to things like "completed classwork" and "handed in homework." The goal card was still an efficient way for the teacher and us to communicate.

Homework can be dreadful for a student with attention deficits or hyperactivity. Those who take medication, like Brian, no longer benefit from it by evening. Some nights Brian would be so rattled and fidgety that he could hardly do fifteen minutes of homework. I made a pact with the fifth-grade teacher that Brian would do as much as he— and I—could tolerate. If Brian was struggling too much on any given night, I could call it quits. I would send a note to the teacher the next day, so he would know that Brian had tried, and the teacher would usually give him extra time to work on it. We agreed that the focus for Brian should be on doing *quality* work and learning while doing rather than on the *quantity* of problems done.

Because of his need for speech therapy, Brian received services at school through the category of "exceptional educational needs" (EEN). Each year a team of regular and special education teachers and an administrator met with us to develop Brian's individualized educational plan (IEP). This plan identified his strengths and weaknesses and established annual and short-term goals that could be addressed in the regular class or through special education teachers or other personnel. In grades K–4, he didn't require any special education services besides that. At our regularly scheduled team meeting at the beginning of fifth grade, a staff member mentioned that Brian would benefit from occupational therapy (OT). He still struggled with fine-motor skills (tying shoes, buttoning, using scissors were still difficult), and he performed most large-motor tasks with a mixed-hand dominant approach. I would never have thought of requesting OT and am very grateful that that service was provided. Because of the existence of an IEP, it has also been easier to insist on and receive guidance services for Brian.

Brian's struggle to manipulate a pencil impaired his efforts to produce schoolwork. It was difficult to get him to write more than a short paragraph or two. So we began to use a word processor. Brian would recite what he wanted to say, and I would type it out, verbatim. When he was freed of the physical and cognitive efforts required to produce written work, his stories showed a creative, comical aspect that we had rarely seen in him. He was soon doing his own typing. He still produced less work than most of his classmates, but what he typed was more and better than what he had been doing before. I have learned to notice such small signs of progress and hold on to them for hope of more to come.

After a successful fifth-grade year, Brian entered middle school with some confidence (Mark and I, however, were nervous!). The year began well enough and continued without major incident until the second semester. Brian was taking an accelerated math class and had received grades of B and A- for the first two quarters. During the third quarter the class covered geometry, word problems, and other abstract concepts that many with ADHD have difficulty with. Brian's quarter grade dropped to a D. Ironically, that same quarter Brian took a state math test, given only to students in accelerated classes, and scored higher than any sixth grader from his school for the previous two years! In the last quarter he again earned a B. Children with ADHD can be as unpredictable in their academic performance as they are in their behavior.

At this time, several students were hassling Brian regularly. He was being teased by other students about his speech, which still needed remediation for articulation errors. And he still had no friend to boost his spirits and counteract those episodes, which crushed his already low self-esteem. He began to show signs of depression and anxiety. Some childhood fears resurfaced, especially fear of the dark. We kept in touch with his psychologist and the guidance counselor at school; his difficulties continued until the end of the school year. Summer, as usual, was a respite for Brian; he could stay home and read or do puzzles, without peers or class schedules to pressure him.

He joined a summer ball league, which pleased Mark and me, and yet we were nervous about what might transpire. In previous years, Brian had remained on the sidelines, in both the physical and the social senses. That year, however, he was slightly more assertive, and his skill levels were good enough that the other boys accepted him quite well. The group went on to win the championship and developed a true team spirit. It was wonderful to watch Brian being a part of that; he even joined them at their end-of-the-season swimming party.

But when school started again, he made no attempt to reestablish contact with those team members. He remained mostly a loner. A few boys were friendly to him, but when I offered (and sometimes insisted) on his arranging a contact, he was not willing to risk being rejected.

Brian still had many helpful teachers in middle school, but we ran into more resistance than during the elementary years. A few teachers told me straight out that they thought this disorder was only an excuse and that Brian needed to learn responsibility for himself. Mark and I agreed, he did need to learn responsibility, but those with ADHD *need more time and more guidance* than most students.

With Brian approaching adolescence, it became difficult to give him the help he needed and still respect his new resistance to our suggestions. I now did more advocating "behind the scenes"—promoting self-reliance to Brian yet asking the teachers to keep track of him and let us know of any concerns. (A few were wonderful enough to call when he was doing well!)

Brian had a hard time organizing his time and his materials. He frequently forgot to go to band lessons or speech therapy, things that were not part of his daily routine. He also forgot to go to the office for his medication. I asked that someone in the school remind him but was told that he needed to be responsible for that himself. Self-reliance is our goal for Brian, but it seems to me absurd to refuse to remind a student about the medication he was prescribed in part because he can't remember what he should do!

Brian's school required seventh-grade students to use an assignment notebook. Organizational aids like this help all students but are necessary for those with ADHD to succeed. Mark and I would check Brian's backpack each night, but we could only follow through on what he had remembered to write down or bring home. I asked his teachers to let me know when any work was missing. Some teachers did call; others did not. One of those teachers who did not call surprised me instead at conference time with the news that Brian was missing five assignments, all recorded as zeros in the grade book. So he was getting an F for the quarter grade, despite a B average on tests. I was concerned, because had we known about the missing work ahead of time, as we had tried to arrange, that F could have been avoided. I discussed this jointly with the teacher, the guidance counselor, and the vice principal, and the F was changed to an Incomplete. We agreed that this way he would be held accountable for still doing all of the work. That evening I had Brian empty his folder and look through his book, and we found all but one of those assignments, completely done but not handed in. This sort of thing is frustrating and hard to understand but is common among students with ADHD.

In seventh grade, Brian began to be argumentative and act frustrated at home, much like he had in earlier years. He was dealing with a double whammy—ADHD plus puberty! He finally decided to assert himself at school and stand up to those who continued to torment him. But those students knew they could get Brian rattled until he struck out and became the one who got into trouble. Brian served a few in-school detentions for incidents of shoving and kicking. We took away privileges at home and reminded him that no matter what others say or do, it is not proper to hurt them. He was also commended by us and school staff for being honest about his involvement and for serving his detention respectfully. We reminded him that he should talk to a teacher or counselor if he was having problems. He did approach two of them, and we praised him for taking action and being willing to discuss his concerns.

Brian can be as delightful as he can be difficult. His humor is subtle but witty. And fortunately for Mark and me (who get discouraged and yell more than we should), he is very forgiving.

He learns easily, but his knowledge is not always available to produce work at the time and in the way it is assigned. Sometimes he cannot focus on the task at hand; other times he is so "tuned in" that we can hardly pull him away. Besides difficulty with sustained attention, students with ADHD have difficulty with selective attention. Brian might miss the main point of a lecture but remember dates and details that most students never noticed.

We've been fortunate that in our schools, most teachers have been supportive. Many parents of ADHD children that I know have not been so fortunate. Some teachers will not even acknowledge the legitimacy of the disorder, much less accommodate the student's unique learning style.

Brian continues to struggle with things that plague most students with attention deficits: lost or forgotten assignments, poorly organized work, confusion over directions, and much variability in performance. Mark and I work hard at trying to help him learn the needed skills without doing tasks for him. So far the burden has been heavy, but each time we see Brian reaching out from his old habits just a bit, we feel pride in him and know that someday it will all be worthwhile. Those teachers that are perceptive and sensitive to Brian's individuality and willing to work with us make all the difference in the world, not just in Brian's schooling, but in lightening the load that we carry in trying to help him be the best he can be.

CHAPTER 2

Overview of ADHD

Attention-deficit/hyperactivity disorder is one of the most intriguing, beguiling, and complicated topics in the field of education. It is also recognized as one of the most common childhood disorders. The condition has had a fascinating history and remains controversial today, in great part, because professional perspectives and personal opinions vary greatly regarding the nature and treatment of ADHD. Nevertheless, the last few years have witnessed an increased awareness of and activity regarding this disorder.

The intent of this book is to present useful techniques, suggestions, and guidelines for addressing the needs of students with ADHD who are in school. The book is designed primarily for teachers (special and general education) and other school-based personnel who provide direct or indirect services to this group. The content of this chapter provides background information for understanding ADHD so that meaningful applications to classroom situations can be made. Specifically, this chapter defines what ADHD is, explains the legal implications for needed services, describes the presumed causes of the condition, highlights select educationally relevant features associated with ADHD, addresses important issues related to the disorder, and introduces a model for conceptualizing the multiple nature of intervention.

Definitional Perspective

Attention-deficit/hyperactivity disorder is an invisible developmental disability that affects a significant number of individuals. As a developmental disability, it can be identified in childhood, continue into adulthood, result in significant problems in many functional life activities, and require certain services. For students, functional limitations will be reflected in difficulty with an assortment of school-related activities, including academic and nonacademic activities. ADHD is a hidden disability because there are no specific physical characteristics associated with the condition; it is only through behavioral manifestations that it becomes recognizable.

A Brief Historical Chronology

As Lerner and Lerner (1991) suggest, various terms have been used throughout the fifty years that the condition has been reported in the literature. Currently, the term *attention-deficit/hyperactivity disorder* is being used most frequently in the United States. This terminology is used in the *Diagnostic and Statistical Manual of Mental Disorders,* fourth edition (*DSM–IV,* 1994), the most frequently cited reference on this condition. For a global perspective, the World Health Organization's *International Classification of Diseases,* tenth edition (*ICD–10*), published in 1992, is typically used and promotes the term *hyperkinetic disorders* to describe conditions related to problems in attention and hyperactivity.

Regardless of the term used, fundamentally, the condition referred to includes problems in attention, impulsivity, and hyperactivity. The predominance of any one of these features in the classification system used during a given period of time is a function of the professional tag at that time. The evolution of terminology and meanings associated with the concept of attention-deficit/hyperactivity disorder is outlined in Table 2.1. The table, an updated adaptation of a table developed by Lerner and Lerner (1991), illustrates how professional thinking has changed over the last five decades as reflected in professional resources.

DSM–IV Diagnostic Criteria

According to the fourth edition of the *Diagnostic and Statistical Manual of Mental Disorders,* ADHD is a disruptive disorder characterized by persistent patterns and inappropriate degrees of inattention and/or hyperactivity-impulsivity. These principal features distinguish ADHD from other disruptive disorders such as conduct disorder (i.e., physical fighting) and oppositional defiant behavior (i.e., recurrent pattern of disobedience).

Table 2.1

Historical Overview of Attention-Deficit/Hyperactivity Disorder

Date	Diagnostic Terminology	Source	Characteristics
1941, 1947	Brain damage syndrome	Werner & Strauss (1941), Strauss & Lehtinen (1947)	Hyperactivity, distractibility, impulsivity, emotionality, unstable perseveration
1962	Minimal brain dysfunction	Clements & Peters	Soft neurological indicators, specific learning deficits, hyperkinesis, impulsivity, short attention span
1968	Hyperkinetic reaction of childhood	DSM–II	Hyperactivity
1980	Attention deficit disorder with hyperactivity (ADDH)	DSM–III	(a) Inattention, impulsivity, motor hyperactivity (b) Onset before age 7 (c) Duration of at least 6 months
	Attention deficit disorder without hyperactivity		Inattention, disorganization, difficulty completing tasks
1987	Attention-deficit hyperactivity disorder (ADHD)	DSM–III-R	Any 8 of a set of 14 symptoms
	Undifferentiated attention deficit disorder (U-ADD)		Developmentally inappropriate and marked inattention

(Continues)

Table 2.1 (Continued)

Date	Diagnostic Terminology	Source	Characteristics
1992	Hyperkinetic disorders	ICD–10	Early onset (before 6 years of age)
			Combination of overactive, poorly modulated behavior with marked inattention and lack of persistent task involvement
			Pervasiveness over situations and persistence over time (at least 6 months)
1994	Attention deficit/hyperactivity disorder	DSM–IV	Either: 6 or more of 9 *inattention* symptoms
			Or: 6 or more of 9 *hyperactivity-impulsivity* symptoms
			Persists for at least 6 months
			Maladaptive and inconsistent with development level
			Some impairment from symptoms present in 2 or more settings

Note. Adapted from "Attention Deficit Disorder: Issues and Questions," by J. W. Lerner and S. R. Lerner, 1991, *Focus on Exceptional Children, 24,* p. 6. Copyright 1991 by Love Publishing Company. Adapted with permission.

The major criteria contained in the *DSM–IV* are likely to guide diagnostic practice in the near future. The final criteria evolved from extensive committee work and changed throughout the process of revision. According to the *DSM–IV*, ADHD can be one of four types that are based on two sets of symptoms. The diagnostic criteria for ADHD are presented in Figure 2.1.

Based on the criteria listed in Figure 2.1, the following four types of ADHD are possible:

- attention-deficit/hyperactivity disorder, combined type
- attention-deficit/hyperactivity disorder, predominantly inattentive type
- attention-deficit/hyperactivity disorder, predominantly hyperactive-impulsive type
- attention-deficit/hyperactivity disorder not otherwise specified

Teachers should be familiar with the symptoms associated with the criteria listed in Figure 2.1 and with the different types of ADHD. Since the diagnosis of ADHD typically occurs in noneducational settings by psychologists or medical personnel, students so identified will bring with them a dossier of information about their condition that most likely will be based on *DSM–IV* criteria.

Prevalence of ADHD

Estimates of the existence of attention-deficit/hyperactivity disorder in the school-age population range from conservative figures under 2% to liberal ones of 30%. These extreme variations in estimated prevalence rates reflect the lack of an exact definition and problems in identification. Nevertheless, even conservative estimates suggest that a substantial number of students may have this condition.

Legal Bases for Service Delivery and Protection

Individuals with Disabilities Education Act of 1990 (IDEA), P.L. 101-476

Students with attention-deficit/hyperactivity disorder may be served under IDEA; however, it is not a separate disability category in this law. In 1991, the U.S. Department of Education (DOE) issued a Policy

---

DSM–IV Diagnostic Criteria for
Attention-Deficit/Hyperactivity Disorder

A. Either (1) or (2):

    (1) six (or more) of the following symptoms of inattention have persisted for at least 6 months to a degree that is maladaptive and inconsistent with developmental level:

Inattention

    (a) often fails to give close attention to details or makes careless mistakes in schoolwork, work, or other activities

    (b) often has difficulty sustaining attention in tasks or play activities

    (c) often does not seem to listen when spoken to directly

    (d) often does not follow through on instructions and fails to finish schoolwork, chores, or duties in the workplace (not due to oppositional behavior or failure to understand instructions)

    (e) often has difficulty organizing tasks and activities

    (f) often avoids, dislikes, or is reluctant to engage in tasks that require sustained mental effort (such as schoolwork or homework)

    (g) often loses things necessary for tasks or activities (e.g., toys, school assignments, pencils, books, or tools)

    (h) is often easily distracted by extraneous stimuli

    (i) is often forgetful in daily activities

    (2) six (or more of the following symptoms of hyperactivity-impulsivity have persisted for at least 6 months to a degree that is maladaptive and inconsistent with developmental level:

Hyperactivity

    (a) often fidgets with hands or feet or squirms in seat

    (b) often leaves seat in classroom or in other situations in which remaining seated is expected

    (c) often runs about or climbs excessively in situations in which it is inappropriate (in adolescents or adults, may be limited to subjective feelings of restlessness)

Figure 2.1. *DSM–IV* diagnostic criteria for attention-deficit/hyperactivity disorder. *Note.* From *Diagnostic and Statistical Manual of Mental Disorders* (4th ed., pp. 83–85), by American Psychiatric Association, 1994, Washington, DC: Author. Copyright 1994 by the American Psychiatric Association. Reprinted with permission.

  (d) often has difficulty playing or engaging in leisure activities quietly

  (e) is often "on the go" or often acts as if "driven by a motor"

  (f) often talks excessively

 Impulsivity

  (g) often blurts out answers before questions have been completed

  (h) often has difficulty awaiting turn

  (i) often interrupts or intrudes on others (e.g., butts into conversations or games)

B. Some hyperactive-impulsive or inattentive symptoms that caused impairment were present before age 7 years.

C. Some impairment from the symptoms is present in two or more settings (e.g., at school [or work] and at home).

D. There must be clear evidence of clinically significant impairment in social, academic, or occupational functioning.

E. The symptoms do not occur exclusively during the course of a pervasive developmental disorder, schizophrenia, or other psychotic disorder and are not better accounted for by another mental disorder (e.g., mood disorder, anxiety disorder, dissociative disorder, or a personality disorder).

Code based on type:

314.01 Attention-Deficit/Hyperactivity Disorder, Combined Type: if both Criteria A1 and A2 are met for the past 6 months.

314.00 Attention-Deficit/Hyperactivity Disorder, Predominantly Inattentive Type: if Criterion A1 is met but Criterion A2 is not met for the past 6 months.

314.01 Attention-Deficit/Hyperactivity Disorder, Predominantly Hyperactive-Impulsive Type: if Criterion A2 is met but Criterion A1 is not met for the past 6 months.

Coding note: For individuals (especially adolescents and adults) who currently have symptoms that no longer meet full criteria, "in partial remission" should be specified.

314.9 Attention-Deficit/Hyperactivity Disorder Not Otherwise Specified: for disorders with prominent symptoms of inattention or hyperactivity-impulsivity that do not meet criteria for attention-deficit/hyperactivity disorder.

Figure 2.1. Continued.

Memorandum indicating that students with "attention deficit disorder" (the terminology used by DOE) who need special education and/or related services can qualify for such services under existing categories. Students whose primary disability is ADHD are eligible under the category "Other Health Impaired" (OHI). This category includes all chronic and acute conditions that result in limited alertness and adversely affect educational performance. In general, this disability category is not being utilized as a way of qualifying students with ADHD for special services (Reid, Maag, & Vasa, 1994).

Students whose primary disability is not ADHD, although they display the symptoms outlined in Figure 2.1, may be likely to qualify under other categories. For instance, in their school-based study of students who displayed characteristics of ADHD and were receiving special education services, Reid and colleagues (1994) found that nearly 52% were identified as behaviorally disordered, 29% were identified officially as learning disabled, and 9% were identified as mentally retarded. In other words, a substantial number of students with ADHD who qualify for services under IDEA will likely qualify under the categories of behavior disorders and learning disabilities.

Often certain behaviors manifested by students with ADHD lead to different perceptions of their disabling condition. A classroom behavior that is often misinterpreted by teachers is what looks like noncompliance. As Goldstein and Goldstein (1990) point out, what is often seen as purposeful noncompliance is actually better viewed as a lack of competence. In other words, many students with ADHD will seem to defy teacher directives when in fact they really are not able to react in a competent way. The misreading of noncompliance and the likely punishment that follows it create problems for students who are not really trying to defy their teachers. For this reason, it is important that teachers be aware of this phenomenon and be able to distinguish between the two behaviors.

Prior to the U.S. Department of Education's (1991) policy many professionals in the field of learning disabilities assumed that students with attention-deficit/hyperactivity disorder who were experiencing significant problems in school were meeting eligibility requirements for learning disabilities and therefore receiving services. In reality, however, only approximately 50% of those students with ADHD were qualifying for special education services. Preceding the reauthorization of IDEA in 1990, the often heated discussion that focused on whether ADHD should be a separate disability category drew attention to this underserved group of students.

Over the last few years, many professionals have come to realize that a sizable number of students with ADHD were floundering in school and not qualifying for services that might be beneficial to them. As a result, changes in professional thinking toward services for students with ADHD have occurred. Unfortunately, such changes do not always result in best practice.

Section 504 of the Rehabilitation Act of 1973 (P.L. 93-112)

In the past, some students with ADHD, albeit not many, have qualified for services under Section 504 of the Rehabilitation Act. The intent of the law as it applies to schools is to provide general or special education and related aids and services that are designed to meet the individual educational needs of those with disabilities as adequately as the needs of those who are not disabled. This is not a "special education" law, but rather a civil rights law that covers the entire educational system.

Section 504 includes a larger group of people who are disabled and differs in some respects from IDEA. This law protects all students who have disabilities, defined as any physical or mental impairment that substantially limits one or more major life activity. Since one of the stated life activities is learning, it becomes obvious that it also applies to schools. If a school has reason to believe that a student has a disability as defined under Section 504, the school must evaluate the student. If it is determined that the student is disabled under this law, then the school must develop and implement a plan for the delivery of services that are needed (Council of Administrators of Special Education, 1992). However, a written IEP is not required.

If a student with ADHD cannot qualify for services under IDEA, qualification might be possible under Section 504. However, many of the substantive and procedural components found in IDEA are either different or missing in Section 504. Nevertheless, Section 504 provides another avenue for accommodating the needs of students with ADHD in schools. Figure 2.2 provides a flow chart of how both IDEA and Section 504 function relative to a possible diagnosis of ADHD.

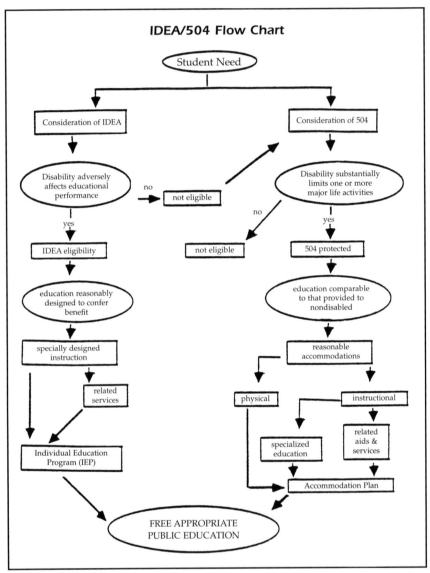

Figure 2.2. IDEA/504 flow chart. *Note.* From *Student Access: A Resource Guide for Educators: Section 504 of the Rehabilitation Act of 1973* (p. 3a), by Council of Administrators of Special Education, 1992, Reston, VA: Author. Copyright 1992 by Council of Administrators of Special Education. Reprinted with permission.

Causes of ADHD

Like the majority of other developmental disabilities of students in school, the precise etiology of ADHD typically is not known or cannot be specified. However, most professionals agree that it is a neurologically based condition. Whether the exact causes are neuroanatomical (a function of brain structure), neurochemical (a function of chemical imbalance), neurophysiological (to do with brain function), or some combination of these is still being investigated. As a result, neurological evidence for explaining ADHD is not yet available (Riccio, Hynd, Cohen, & Gonzalez, 1993).

Some data exist to suggest that genetics may play a role in ADHD. Studies have shown a familial association of various features associated with the disorder. Parents and siblings of children with ADHD have higher rates of ADHD than would be expected. Certain neurological conditions may be transmitted genetically that predispose an individual to attention and hyperactive problems. Although parents often feel a need to understand why, the etiology is really not relevant to medical treatment or educational strategies.

General Features of ADHD

Placement Realities

Most students with ADHD are in general education classrooms and do not need to be removed from those settings. However, certain accommodations may need to be made to address their needs. Reid and colleagues (1994) found that the great majority of students with ADHD who were receiving special education services were in general education most, or all, of their school day.

That most students are in general education suggests that classroom teachers need to understand this condition and know how to deal with it in their classrooms. Special educators must be prepared to collaborate with general educators in this venture and must know how to modify curriculum, instruction, and assignments. General education and special education teachers will also need to be competent managers of behavior and to be adept at teaching students how to manage their own behavior.

Classroom Manifestations

The specific characteristics of ADHD that manifest themselves in the classroom can vary greatly. Recognizing and knowing how to accommodate them are the challenges that confront teachers. A general sense of what behavior might arise in classroom settings is available from examining the *DSM–IV* criteria. Behaviors that might be associated with ADHD and manifest in classroom settings can be grouped into the following categories: attention and concentration, reasoning and information processing, memory, executive functions (e.g., planning and organizing actions), social and emotional areas, communication, and academic performance. These areas and associated behaviors are discussed in the next chapter.

Most of the suggested ways for accommodating each presenting behavior involve relatively minor modifications and can be accomplished easily. The payoff for taking the time to make these accommodations is well worth the effort. Specific techniques for addressing various classroom manifestations of ADHD are covered in Chapters 4–6.

Attainment/Outcome Data

As mentioned previously, ADHD may continue throughout adulthood. It is quite possible that the primary characteristics associated with the condition (e.g., impulsivity) will continue to be problematic for the individual. Furthermore, the residual effects of previous problems (e.g., social or emotional problems) associated with ADHD may linger. Either possibility can have a profound effect on the adult life of an individual with ADHD.

Much of what is known about the adult status of individuals with ADHD comes from followup studies. The literature reveals that a significant portion of those who have ADHD will have difficulty dealing with the demands of adulthood. As Goldstein and Goldstein (1990) state, "The years of ADHD problems certainly take their toll on adult outcomes" (p. 25). They also note that successful adult adjustment is affected by the following general variables: intelligence, socioeconomic status, socialization, activity level, ability to delay rewards, aggression, and family mental health.

School-Based Model of Intervention

Even though it has been established that ADHD is not just a childhood condition, it is also true that most intervention efforts, when they are implemented, occur in school settings. This is not to suggest that adult issues are not as important.

A school-based approach to addressing the needs of students with ADHD must be comprehensive to assure appropriateness. A model of educational intervention that covers a full range of target areas is depicted in Figure 2.3. This model is built on four fundamental intervention areas: environmental management, instructional accommodations, student-regulated strategies, and medical management. It also contains two mediating variables (assessment procedures and program planning and collaboration) that influence how the four major areas are involved. A brief explanation of the four major intervention areas follows.

Environmental Management

Environmental management (see Chapter 4) relates closely to the concept of classroom management, which can be defined as "all teacher-directed activities that support the efficient operations of the classroom and lead to the establishment of optimal conditions for learning and order" (Smith, Polloway, Patton, & Dowdy, 1995, p. 350). Changes to the classroom setting and implementation of behavior management systems are examples of environmental management.

Classroom or environmental management is made up of seven dimensions, all of which should be considered when addressing the needs of students with ADHD. The following are various management dimensions and select examples that relate to students with ADHD:

- psychosocial: student, teacher, peer, family factors
- physical: arrangement of classroom, seating, assistive technology
- instructional: scheduling, transitions, grouping, lesson planning, homework
- procedural: classroom rules and procedures
- behavioral: creating and increasing desirable behaviors, decreasing undesirable behaviors, generalizing and maintaining behaviors

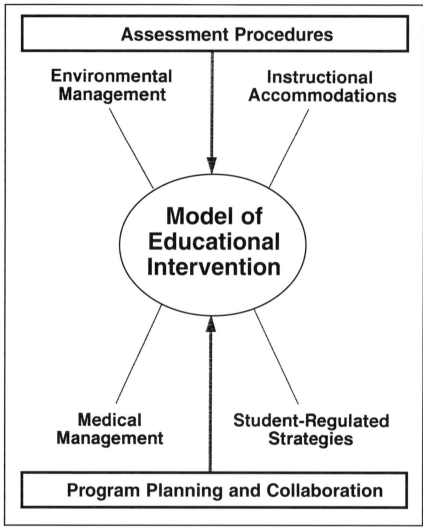

Figure 2.3. Model of educational intervention.

- involvement of personnel: teaching assistants, peer tutors, volunteers
- work environment of teacher, instructional applications

A working understanding and proper application of behavior management principles are extremely important. Emphasis should be on the use of positive reinforcement and movement toward a system in which students regulate their own behaviors.

Instructional Accommodations

Students with ADHD may benefit greatly from certain accommodations that can be made to their instructional programs (see Chapter 5). Such accommodations can involve curriculum, materials, instructional processes, and the products students produce as a result of instruction. Examples of accommodations that may be appropriate for students with ADHD include:

- curriculum: providing life, study, and social skills instruction

- materials: using a variety of media, advanced organizers, multi-level materials, graphic aids, highlighting

- processes: allowing active involvement of student in the lesson; using demonstration / guided practice / independent practice paradigm; giving clear directions; using cooperative learning situations; making adaptations regarding speed, accuracy, and amount of assigned work

- products: allowing alternative final products, portfolios; making testing accommodations, grading considerations

Student-Regulated Strategies

Student-regulated strategies, though initially taught by the teacher, can be viewed as interventions that are intended to be implemented independently by the students (see Chapter 6). Characteristically, students with ADHD display certain behaviors (e.g., various attentional problems) for which self-regulatory interventions (e.g., self-monitoring) are appropriate and warranted. These strategies offer the promise of enhancing the educational development of students with ADHD by:

- increasing selective attention/focus

- modifying impulsive responding

- providing verbal mediators to assist in academic and social problem-solving situations

- teaching effective self-instructional statements to enable students to "talk through" tasks and problems

- providing strategies that may lead to improvement in peer relations and the development of prosocial behaviors (Rooney, 1995)

Medical Management

Although school personnel are not involved in the prescription of medication for students with ADHD, they do play an important role in its usage (see Chapter 7). Monitoring students who are on medication is probably the most critical aspect of being part of the treatment team. It is essential that school personnel communicate with parents and physicians regarding the effects of the medications that a student is taking.

The most commonly used medication is methylphenidate (the brand name is Ritalin), which is a mild stimulant. Studies have indicated that 84% to 93% of medical professionals who prescribe medication for children with ADHD select this drug. Another medication used with children with ADHD is premoline (the brand name is Cylert).

The medications prescribed to address the behaviors associated with ADHD have a number of possible outcomes, ranging from positive to negative. Some of the desirable outcomes of using medication with students who have ADHD are increased attention, improved academic performance, and increased appropriate behaviors. Some of the negative outcomes include weight loss, irritability, behavior swings, nausea, organ damage, and dizziness. Everyone involved with the treatment program must be alert to all of these factors and willing to make adjustments as necessary.

Final Thoughts

Attention-deficit/hyperactivity disorder is a condition that has been on the forefront of the public education issue for several years, but it remains illusive. ADHD continues to mystify professionals, families, and those who have it. From a school perspective, students with ADHD present a real challenge, as they often encounter problems in many phases of the education process. From an adult perspective, the same characteristics, plus the baggage that comes with living with these problems for many years, can have a significant effect on major life functions. For these reasons, we must take this condition seriously and strive to do the following:

- create accommodative environments in which people with ADHD can thrive
- teach self-regulatory behaviors that create independence
- provide appropriate supports, as needed
- link individuals with requisite services
- ensure that collaborative efforts guide service delivery

CHAPTER 3

Assessing ADHD for Classroom Purposes

The assessment and diagnosis of attention-deficit/hyper-activity disorder traditionally has been the responsibility of psychologists, psychiatrists, and physicians. However, a recent interpretation of Section 504 of P.L. 93-112, the Vocational Rehabilitation Act Amendments of 1973, by the assistant secretary for civil rights (Cantu, 1993) suggests that public education personnel clearly have responsibilities in this area of assessment. Under Section 504, if a school district suspects that a child has a disability that substantially limits a major life activity, such as learning, the school district is obligated to evaluate. If the disability is confirmed through assessment, the school district must provide services. Attention-deficit/hyperactivity disorder has been accepted as a disability that may substantially limit learning; therefore, a child suspected of having an attention deficit is eligible for assessment and services provided by the school district.

If parents make the request for assessment for attention-deficit/hyperactivity disorder and the school does not believe that the child is in need of special education and related services or regular education with supplementary services, the school may refuse to assess. In that case, however, the parents must be informed that they have the right to challenge the school's decision through due process procedures. Other Section 504 safeguards for parents include permission to challenge the positive identification of attention deficit, notification of placement decisions, right to review records, right to an impartial hearing, right to have legal counsel, and right for review (Cantu, 1993).

Although teachers are not directly responsible for assessing attention deficits, there are several reasons to include assessment information in a resource for teachers. Section 504 requires that school personnel be trained to adequately evaluate and serve children with ADHD. Since teachers may be the first to suspect the disability, it is critical for them to have a basic knowledge of widely used assessment techniques and of specific behaviors to look for when deciding whether to refer a child for more in-depth evaluation. Since teachers will participate on the interdisciplinary team that reviews assessment data for identification and program planning, they should be informed consumers of this information. Teachers are also frequently called upon to administer or respond to assessment instruments that will be considered, along with parental input, as key information in determining the existence of ADHD.

Atkins and Pelham (1991) suggest several factors that make teachers an important source of information in the assessment of attention deficit:

- Teachers spend a significant amount of time with students.

- Teachers observe students across a variety of academic and social tasks.

- Teachers are relatively objective as compared to parents.

- Teachers have opportunities to observe age, sex, and grade-appropriate behavior in a large peer group.

- Teachers base their recommendations on numerous observations of the student in various natural environments.

- Research has demonstrated that teachers are able to differentiate between students with and without symptoms of attention deficit.

Atkins and Pelham offer a caution regarding the exclusive use of teacher-based assessment because of the global and subjective nature of these reports. Teachers have also been found to be more likely to rate a student as hyperactive and inattentive if the student has been defiant toward them (Schachar, Sandberg, & Rutter, 1986). Because all individuals have different tolerance levels for specific behaviors, multiple sources should be used and multiple assessment procedures employed.

When the assessment process begins, teachers and other school personnel may be asked to relay their opinions and observations through a variety of formats. They may be interviewed regarding their informal observations of attention-deficit–like characteristics, or they may be asked to complete a formal or informal rating scale. Input from school personnel is critical at various points throughout the identification and intervention process.

A model identification and intervention process has been described by Burnley (1993) in a four-part plan that could be used to structure the efforts of an interdisciplinary team in each school. A modified version of Burnley's process is depicted in Figure 3.1.

Following is a summary of each step with recommendations and options that may be considered for implementation in a school district. The purpose of this chapter is to provide a general overview of the school's responsibility for assessing ADHD and to identify commonly used assessment techniques and instruments. More formal study would be necessary to become a trained specialist in the diagnosis of ADHD.

Step 1: Preliminary Assessment and Initial Child-Study Meeting

Preliminary Assessment

Each teacher should have access to a copy of the *Diagnostic and Statistical Manual of Mental Disorders,* fourth edition (*DSM–IV*) criteria and should be trained in identifying the characteristics (listed in Figure 2.1) that may be manifested in the classroom. When teachers observe that several of the *DSM–IV* behaviors are characteristic of one student, note that the behaviors are interfering with success in the classroom, and determine that the behaviors are significantly different than those of the student's peers, they should begin to keep a two-week behavioral observation log. The log should document the child's attention-deficit–like behaviors and the times during which the behaviors appear to be more intense, occur more frequently, or are of longer duration. The specific classroom activities should also be noted, including the academic task and the type of activity (e.g., independent or group work). Figure 3.2 provides a form that may be used to structure the development of the teacher's observation log. If the teacher's observations continue to reflect significant attention-deficit–like behaviors, the school district's referral process should be initiated. The observation log should be attached to the referral.

**ADHD Process for
Identification and Intervention**

STEP 1

Preliminary Assessment

Initial Child-Study Team Meeting

STEP 2

Formal Assessment

Follow-up Meeting of Child-Study Team

STEP 3

Collaborative Meeting for Strategy Development

STEP 4

Follow-up and Progress Review

Figure 3.1. ADHD process for identification and intervention. *Note.* Developed from "A Team Approach for Identification of an Attention Deficit Hyperactivity Disorder Child," by C. D. Burnley, 1993, *The School Counselor,* 40, pp. 228–230.

Classroom Observation for Attention-Deficit Behaviors

Teacher:_____ School:_____

Child:_____ Grade:_____ Age:_____

Class Activity	Child's Behavior	Date/Time

Figure 3.2. Sample form for documenting classroom manifestations of attention-deficit–like behaviors.

The school counselor or other school personnel trained in observation techniques should also observe the child in the classroom to provide comparative information. Direct observation has the advantage of allowing data collection in the student's natural environment. Information gathered is also considered less biased than responses obtained in interviews, in which leading questions may be asked (Schaughency & Rothlind, 1991). Several formats are available to structure this observation. One of the most frequently cited and simple to use is the TOAD (Talking out, Out of seat, Attention problem, Disruption) system (Goldstein & Goldstein, 1990). The TOAD system facilitates the collection of data on four of the most frequently problematic behaviors for children with ADHD. Following is a list of the behaviors and the operational definition of each.

Talking out: The child is speaking directly to either the teacher, without first obtaining permission to speak, or classmates, when unsolicited and during inappropriate times or work periods.

Out of seat: The child's weight is not being supported by the chair. Sitting on knees does not count as out-of-seat behavior.

Attention problem: The child is not attending either to a group activity or to independent work. The child is engaged in an activity other than that directed by the teacher and is clearly different from what the other students are doing. This includes the child not following the teacher's directions.

Disruption: The child's actions appear to be interrupting other students' work. These actions might include physical contact or noises. They may be intentional or unintentional.

The observer should use a timer to observe the child for periods of fifteen, thirty, forty-five, or sixty seconds at regular intervals (e.g., every thirty minutes). All four behaviors are looked for at the same time. Only one notation is made regardless of the number of times the behavior might be observed during each period. At the end of the observation, the number of observations noted is totaled for each behavior and divided by the total number of observation points. This will provide the percentage of negative observations for each behavior. For example, if 128 periods were observed and the child was not attending during 64 of the periods, the nonattending behavior would be 50%. The authors suggest that each school system obtain local norms for the most beneficial use of this data. Figure 3.3 provides a coding sheet that may be used for the TOAD system.

TOAD System

Child: _____ Date: _____

Teacher: _____ Time Begin: _____ Time End: _____

Activity: _____ Location: _____

Observer: _____ Time period: ☐ 15 sec.   ☐ 30 sec.
                                               ☐ 45 sec.   ☐ 60 sec.

Period	T	O	A	D	Period	T	O	A	D	Period	T	O	A	D	Period	T	O	A	D
1					33					65					97				
2					34					66					98				
3					35					67					99				
4					36					68					100				
5					37					69					101				
6					38					70					102				
7					39					71					103				
8					40					72					104				
9					41					73					105				
10					42					74					106				
11					43					75					107				
12					44					76					108				
13					45					77					109				
14					46					78					110				
15					47					79					111				
16					48					80					112				
17					49					81					113				
18					50					82					114				
19					51					83					115				
20					52					84					116				
21					53					85					117				
22					54					86					118				
23					55					87					119				
24					56					88					120				
25					57					89					121				
26					58					90					122				
27					59					91					123				
28					60					92					124				
29					61					93					125				
30					62					94					126				
31					63					95					127				
32					64					96					128				

Figure 3.3. TOAD system. *Note.* From *Managing Attention Disorder in Children: A Guide for Practitioners*, by S. Goldstein and M. Goldstein, 1990, New York: John Wiley. Copyright 1990 by John Wiley & Sons, Inc. Reprinted with permission.

It should also be noted that concerns and cautions are found in the literature regarding the use of direct observation. Schaughency and Rothlind (1991) point out that this form of data collection is the most costly in terms of professional time. They also warn that significant behaviors that occur on a low frequency may be missed if the observation period is limited. The best policy seems to be the combined use of observation and other multiple types of information gathering that will be discussed later.

Initial Child-Study Meeting

As early as possible the parents should be notified that their child may be experiencing attention problems that affect the learning process. A meeting should be scheduled that includes the significant individuals in the student's life (Burnley, 1993). Often the principal, teacher, parents, and school counselor will comprise this child-study team.

At the meeting, the information gathered from the teacher's log and the counselor's observations should be presented and discussed. Parents should be asked to respond to the concerns presented by the school personnel and to describe their own observations of attention behaviors outside the school setting. The team should reach a consensus as to whether to conduct a more in-depth assessment process. If further assessment is agreed upon, an individual trained in the identification of ADHD should be placed in charge of that process. The *CHADD Educators Manual* (Fowler, 1992) specifies the following characteristics as indicative of a qualified evaluator:

1. has training required to make a differential diagnosis between ADHD and other childhood disorders

2. has experience and knowledge in evaluating the impact of a stressful life and family dynamics on child adjustment

3. has demonstrated understanding regarding racial, cultural, socioeconomic, language, and ethnic factors that may result in bias during the assessment of culturally diverse children

Someone who is based at the school should also be assigned to provide a central contact for the team members and to ensure that the assessment process proceeds in a timely fashion. Parents and teachers should be provided information on how to contact this person in case of further questions or the need to share further information.

Step 2: Formal Assessment Process and Follow-up Meeting of Child-Study Team

At the second meeting of the child-study team, the assessment results are shared, and the team must resolve the difficult question regarding the presence of an attention deficit as a cause of the child's learning problems. Unlike special education categories such as learning disabilities that are covered under IDEA (1990), there are no specific criteria or established school-based assessment models for ADHD. An important decision to be made by each school district is the extent to which *DSM–IV* will be used to structure the assessment process. Traditionally, schools have not depended on this more clinically based type of diagnosis for eligibility in special education; they have tended to develop and use their own policies. The legal mandate for assessment in this area did not specifically include the use of a clinical or psychiatric diagnosis available through *DSM–IV*. However, McBurnett, Lahey, and Pfiffner (1993) suggest that the recent revisions have made the *DSM–IV* more reliable and more predictive of educational impairment and thus more relevant to educational identification. While what criteria are used is left to each school district to determine, the *DSM–IV* criteria described in Chapter 2 should be given serious consideration. These criteria will be used as the standard for diagnosis in this chapter.

Schaughency and Rothlind (1991) identify a series of questions that should be answered during the assessment process; they also recommend methods and appropriate tests or devices that may be used to answer the questions. To facilitate communication between professionals, they recommend that standard diagnostic criteria such as those in the *DSM–IV* classification system be used. The key questions to guide the identification of ADHD include:

1. Does the child meet the criteria in the *DSM–IV?*
2. Does an alternative educational diagnosis or medical condition account for the attention difficulties?

3. Are the behaviors displayed by the child developmentally appropriate? (For example, children with mental retardation should be compared to children with comparable developmental levels.)

4. Do these behaviors impair the child's functioning in home, school, or social relations situations?

A formal assessment process, including a variety of methods, is needed to answer these questions. Interviews, a development history, and intellectual and academic tests will assist in answering the first two questions. Questions three and four may require norm-based behavior-rating scales with multiple informants and documentation of classroom performance or the impact of the child's behaviors in social situations and home life. The following section offers examples of widely accepted techniques used in the documentation of attention deficit.

Formal Assessment Process

As stated earlier, the assessment process should include multiple techniques for gathering information from multiple sources. Atkins and Pelham (1991) suggest that the assessment battery be designed with dual purposes in mind: first, assessment to identity and define attention-deficit–like behaviors in order to justify special services; and, second, assessment to determine the functional deficits to assist in developing an individualized treatment plan. The assessment procedures implemented should also be useful for determining if the child qualifies for special education services under Section 504. Since assessment for attention deficit is the primary focus of this guide, the reader is referred to local school district policy for more information and specific guidelines for special education placement.

The most frequently cited components of a comprehensive assessment battery for identifying attention-deficit behaviors include:

- observations
- interviews with the child, parents, and teacher
- review of school records
- review of intellectual and academic achievement testing
- rating scales completed by the teachers, parents, and possibly peers
- in some cases, a medical examination

Each of these components can contribute important data to the team's decision-making process. Following is a brief review of each component.

Observations

The value of observation data obtained throughout the assessment and intervention process is well documented; observations are conducted in the natural environment and their data are generally more objective than those obtained through interviews and rating scales (Schaughency & Rothlind, 1991). Since recommendations for both informal and more structured techniques for behavioral observation have been described earlier in this chapter, only a few cautions and recommendations will be noted here:

- While all observations are important, at least one person on the assessment team should be trained in observation techniques and in recognizing ADHD symptoms.

- It is important to observe children across a variety of settings and with different individuals. Some teachers automatically make accommodations for students who are struggling in their classrooms. They may place the children in close proximity, encourage frequent breaks, allow more time on assignments, and accept more talking out and interrupting. Also, children may have a favorite subject that is very stimulating to them, and their attending behavior may be significantly better when that subject is being discussed. Variability of performance should be expected in children with ADHD.

- The time period of observation should be adequate and extended over several days if possible. Many children can control their behavior for short periods of time, particularly when a new person, i.e., the observer, is placed in the environment (Wodrich, 1994).

- Disadvantages to the use of observation measures include the possibility that unless the length of observation is adequate, behaviors that occur at a low frequency but have high saliency might be missed. Another disadvantage is that an adequate observation effort has a high cost in professional time (Schaughency & Rothlind, 1991).

Many of the concerns regarding the use of observation data can be balanced through the addition of data from interviews with individuals such as parents and the children themselves.

Interviews

Systematically conducted, structured interviews are an important component of the assessment of ADHD. Interviews are frequently needed from parents, teachers, and the child suspected of having ADHD. According to Wodrich (1994) and Guevremont, DuPaul, and Barkley (1990), topics covered in typical clinical interviews with parents generally include:

- details of referral concerns
- health, psychiatric, and developmental history
- family history
- status of behavior at home
- interpersonal/social development
- school history and previous testing

Montague, McKinney, and Hocutt (1994) and Schaughency and Rothlind (1991) recommend several structured interviews to allow a more standardized method of obtaining the information. Examples can be found in the *Diagnostic Interview for Children and Adolescents* (DICA/DICA-P) (Weiner, Reich, Herjanic, Jung, & Amado, 1987) and the *Diagnostic Interview Schedule for Children* (DISC/DISC-P) (Costello, Edelbrock, & Costello, 1985).

Wodrich (1994) and Guevremont et al. (1990) suggest addressing the following questions about the child during the teacher interview:

- skill level in each academic subject
- class work habits and productivity
- length of attention (especially for monotonous tasks)
- degree of activity on playground and during class
- compliance with rules
- manifestation of conduct problems

- onset, frequency, and duration of inappropriate behavior and the antecedent events
- social skills and peer acceptance

The interview should also include information on any intervention techniques previously used and the special services now contemplated. If appropriate to age, language development, and cognitive ability, interviewing the student can offer additional insight in the assessment process. Guevremont et al. (1990) suggest that during this session, the child might be queried regarding his or her:

- perception of complaints by the teacher and parent
- attitude toward family and school
- relationships with peers

Interviewers might also ask students to describe their three fondest wishes (Wodrich, 1994). This type of question usually stimulates conversation, allows for a language sample, and may provide insight into the child's important feelings and concerns.

Although important information can be obtained during a child's interview, extreme caution is recommended in using the results of such an interview to validate or invalidate the existence of ADHD (Guevremont et al., 1990; Wodrich, 1994). Children may be unable to provide realistic answers to questions due to lack of awareness or a slanted view of reality. They may withhold the truth due to embarrassment or feelings of inadequacy. The level of inattention, activity, and impulsivity displayed during a one-on-one situation may also not be representative of the child's typical response.

Differences in information obtained by informants should not be interpreted as one individual being right and another wrong. They may reflect differences in the child's behavior in different settings or differences in individual perception of the same behaviors. It is important to see the interview data as one source of information to be considered in combination with other sources.

School Record Review

The review of school records is important to obtain evidence of the ongoing symptoms of ADHD, specifically the type of behaviors noted and their frequency, degree, and duration. Teacher notations may also indicate the impact behaviors have had on relationships with adults and peers. If a child has responded more successfully under specific teachers, teaching styles and other variables may be investigated to assist in setting the stage for positive classroom outcomes in the future.

Intellectual and Academic Achievement

While intelligence and achievement tests are not specifically used to identify ADHD, the results of such tests do impact the team's decision regarding eligibility and service delivery. The results of the intelligence test are particularly important in ruling in or out the child's eligibility for services under IDEA (1990) in categories of mental retardation and learning disabilities. The presence of significantly subaverage intellectual functioning would suggest the need for further testing for eligibility for services under the mental retardation category. Generally, if a child qualifies under IDEA, testing for ADHD is not pursued because all placement needs and related services are available under that law.

It should be noted that students with mental retardation can also be diagnosed as having ADHD, if the attention deficit is significantly lower than expected for that level of mental and adaptive behavior functioning (*DSM–IV*, 1994). For example, one of the characteristics of ADHD is failure to finish tasks. In considering that characteristic, the team would have to determine that the behavior was not due to the student's inability to understand the task and to verify that the task was developmentally appropriate.

Similarly, results of intelligence and academic tests are important in determining if a discrepancy exists between ability and academic achievement. Ability is typically predicted through tests of intelligence. In most states the discrepancy between ability and achievement is the primary consideration for eligibility for services for students with learning disabilities.

Intellectual and academic functioning is also an important consideration in determining the most effective intervention plan. Self-monitoring and self-regulation intervention techniques will be more successful with those children with higher cognitive function. Use of contracts and reinforcement alternatives may also be affected by levels of intelligence and academic achievement.

Rating Scales

The purpose of rating scales is to document the presence of ADHD symptoms, evaluate the presence of compelling or multiple diagnoses, and determine the degree of severity (Fowler, 1992). Rating scales have been relied on heavily by evaluators in an effort to quantify the data collection process and to establish some measure of objectivity. However, some bias is still evident, and the team will need to compare responses across informants for consistency and validate responses and observations through interviews and observations.

Since there are numerous rating scales from which to select, each school district must study the purpose, technical features (reliability, validity), and usability of the testing instruments before adoption. A decision must also be made regarding the type of scale needed. Some scales offer a list of items exclusively related to ADHD characteristics, while others are more general and measure a variety of dimensions. Rating scales may also be found that assess situational variables (e.g., home or school), social competence, learning, and ADHD behaviors across informants (Worthington, Patterson, Elliott, & Linkous, 1993).

The *Attention-Deficit/Hyperactivity Disorder Test* (Gilliam, 1995) is an example of a norm-referenced, standardized rating scale that primarily focuses on the diagnosis of ADHD based on *DSM–IV* criteria (American Psychiatric Association, 1994). The test contains three subtests—hyperactivity, impulsivity, and inattention—and is composed of thirty-six items that describe behaviors and characteristics of people with ADHD. The items are based on the most common problems of ADHD as reported in professional literature and *DSM–IV*. The test is designed to be used by parents and professionals and can be used to measure behaviors at school and at home. The behaviors are rated on the basis of the severity of the individual's problem. The data can be used for the identification of other behavioral disorders as well as for diagnosis of ADHD. The test was normed on people ages three to twenty-three and can be administered in approximately five to ten minutes. Figure 3.4 displays a portion of each of the subtests included in the test.

The *Strengths and Limitations Inventory: School Version* (Dowdy, 1996) included in Figure 3.5 is an example of a multidimensional rating scale containing items similar to those used to describe ADHD in *DSM–IV*, in addition to items that address memory, reasoning, executive function, social/emotional status, communication, reading, writing, and math. The SLI is designed to document strengths and limitations that may be manifested in home, academic, or vocational settings. It may be completed by teachers, parents, evaluators, or anyone who has observed the individual over time. The behaviors listed in the SLI are also used in the *Guide to Classroom Interventions* located in Appendix A. This guide provides samples of appropriate interventions for specific behaviors identified in the SLI.

Sample Test Items

	Not a Problem	Mild Problem	Severe Problem
Hyperactivity Subtest			
Is constantly "on the go"	0	1	2
Displays excessive running, jumping, climbing	0	1	2
Displays excessive talking	0	1	2
Has difficulty remaining seated	0	1	2
Is constantly manipulating objects	0	1	2
Impulsivity Subtest			
Acts before thinking	0	1	2
Has difficulty waiting turn	0	1	2
Is impulsive	0	1	2
Interrupts conversations	0	1	2
Does not wait for directions	0	1	2
Inattention Subtest			
Fails to finish projects	0	1	2
Has poor planning ability	0	1	2
Has difficulty following directions	0	1	2
Has difficulty sustaining attention	0	1	2
Has difficulty staying on task	0	1	2

Figure 3.4. Sample test items from *Attention-Deficit/Hyperactivity Disorder Test*. *Note.* From the Summary Response Form of the *Attention-Deficit/Hyperactivity Disorder Test: A Method for Identifying Individuals with ADHD*, by J. G. Gilliam, 1995, Austin, TX: PRO-ED. Copyright 1995 by PRO-ED, Inc. Reprinted with permission.

For example, the assessment of executive function included with the SLI is particularly useful in determining a student's readiness for cognitive intervention strategies. If a student has difficulty with self-monitoring and self-regulation, a behavior management program that is teacher directed may be more successful initially. Intervention in areas of executive function will need to be introduced as self-regulation strategies are implemented for regulating attention-deficit and hyperactivity behaviors.

Table 3.1 contains a list of other frequently used rating scales grouped according to purpose. See Appendix B for complete information on ordering these and other assessment instruments that are appropriate for ADHD. For a more comprehensive review of rating scales and other testing techniques, refer to *Managing Attention Disorders in Children* (Goldstein & Goldstein, 1990) or *Attention Deficit Hyperactivity Disorder* (Barkley, 1990).

Medical Examination

According to *DSM–IV* (American Psychiatric Association, 1994), no laboratory tests have been established to determine the diagnosis of ADHD. It is noted that tests of mental processing have shown differences between children with ADHD and control subjects; however, results have not clearly defined which cognitive deficit is responsible. Likewise, *DSM–IV* states that no specific physical features are associated with ADHD, although it is reported that low-set ears, a high, arched palate, and hypertolerism may occur more frequently in this population.

While they may not be able to specifically rule *in* ADHD, medical examinations are often important in ruling *out* conditions that may be causing the ADHD characteristics; they may also aid in treatment planning. Goldstein and Goldstein (1990) suggest that the physician's role in the assessment process includes:

- identifying any remediable medical cause for the symptoms of ADHD, including anemia, sleep apnea, hyperthyroidism, and side effects from other medication

- determining the need for further medical diagnostic testing, such as a blood count, to exclude a specific illness as the cause of the symptoms of ADHD

- interpreting the results of a physical or neurological examination

Continues on p. 59

Strengths and Limitations Inventory: School Version

Directions: This checklist may be completed during an interview or given to parents, teachers, or other professionals to complete. Informants should check each item according to the frequency of the behavior. Specific examples or comments should be provided when possible. Any characteristic seldom or never observed *may be* considered a strength or ability. Characteristics observed often or very often may pose functional limitations in an academic or vocational setting.

NAME: _____ DATE: _____

COMPLETED BY: _____ RELATIONSHIP TO INDIVIDUAL: _____

Please check each item based on your personal interview, knowledge and/or observation.	No Opportunity to Observe	Never	Sometimes	Often	Very Often	Specific comments, observations, and examples should be provided whenever possible.
I. ATTENTION/IMPULSIVITY/HYPERACTIVITY						
1. Exhibits excessive nonpurposeful movement (can't sit still, stay in seat).						
2. Is easily distracted by auditory stimuli.						
3. Is easily distracted by visual stimuli.						
4. Does not stay on task for appropriate periods of time.						

5. Has difficulty completing assignments.			
6. Verbally or physically interrupts conversations or activities.			
7. Loses place when reading orally.			
8. Sits and does nothing (daydreams).			
9. Rushes through work with little regard for detail (careless).			
10. Does not pay attention to most important stimuli.			
11. Shifts from one uncompleted activity to another.			
12. Does not appear to listen to what is being said.			
13. Talks beyond appropriate limits.			
14. Loses items needed for activities or tasks (paper, pencil, assignments).			
15. Has difficulty working/playing quietly.			
II. REASONING/PROCESSING			
16. Makes poor decisions.			
17. Makes frequent errors.			
18. Has trouble using previously learned information in a new situation.			
19. Has delayed verbal responses.			
20. Takes longer to do a task than peers.			

(Continues)

Figure 3.5. Strengths and Limitations Inventory: School Version.

Strengths and Limitations Inventory: School Version (Continued)

Please check each item based on your personal interview, knowledge and/or observation.	No Opportunity to Observe	Never	Sometimes	Often	Very Often	Specific comments, observations, and examples should be provided whenever possible.
21. Has difficulty adjusting to changes (schedule, personnel, steps in a task, work conditions).						
22. Requires more supervision than peers.						
23. Has difficulty getting started.						
24. Has difficulty understanding social expectations.						
25. Requires concrete demonstrations.						
26. Requires extra practice.						
27. Has difficulty following oral instructions.						
28. Has difficulty following written instructions.						
29. Has difficulty following a map or diagram.						
30. Is disoriented to time, place, purpose.						

III. MEMORY

31. Has difficulty answering questions regarding personal history.

32. Has difficulty repeating information recently heard.

33. Has difficulty repeating information recently read.

34. Has difficulty retaining learned information.

35. Has difficulty following multiple directions.

36. Has difficulty performing tasks in correct sequence.

37. Memory deficits impact daily activities.

IV. EXECUTIVE FUNCTION

38. Has difficulty planning/organizing activities.l

39. Has time management difficulties (attendance, meeting deadlines).

40. Has difficulty setting priorities.

41. Has difficulty attending to several stimuli at once.

42. Has difficulty grasping complex situations.

43. Appears unaware of possible consequences of behavior and personal limitations.

44. Has difficulty inhibiting inappropriate responses.

45. Has difficulty sustaining appropriate behavior for prolonged periods.

46. Has difficulty generating strategies to solve a problem (social, academic, work).

(Continues)

Figure 3.5. Continued.

Strengths and Limitations Inventory: School Version (Continued)

Please check each item based on your personal interview, knowledge and/or observation.

	No Opportunity to Observe	Never	Sometimes	Often	Very Often	Specific comments, observations, and examples should be provided when-ever possible.
47. Has difficulty monitoring own performance throughout activity (self-monitoring).						
48. Has difficulty independently adjusting behavior (self-regulation).						
49. Has difficulty identifying personal strengths and limitations.						
V. INTERPERSONAL SKILLS						
50. Interacts inappropriately with teachers/supervisors of same sex.						
51. Interacts inappropriately with teachers/supervisors of opposite sex.						
52. Responds inappropriately to nonverbal cues.						
53. Uses body language ineffectively.						
54. Uses eye contact ineffectively.						
55. Is verbally aggressive.						
56. Is physically aggressive.						

57. Is withdrawn; avoids social functions.					
58. Has difficulty accepting constructive criticism.					
59. Has difficulty asking for help.					
60. Exhibits signs of poor self-confidence.					

VI. EMOTIONAL MATURITY

61. Displays inappropriate emotions for situation.					
62. Has difficulty accepting new tasks without complaint.					
63. Is frequently upset, irritated.					
64. Displays temper outbursts.					
65. Is easily led by others.					
66. Appears unmotivated.					
67. Does not follow classroom or workplace "rules."					
68. Has difficulty making and keeping friends.					
69. Displays a lack of awareness of social consequences of inappropriate interactions.					
70. Has difficulty working in a group.					
71. Has difficulty working independently.					
72. Has tendency to overreact.					

(Continues)

Figure 3.5. Continued.

Strengths and Limitations Inventory: School Version (Continued)

Please check each item based on your personal interview, knowledge and/or observation.	No Opportunity to Observe	Never	Sometimes	Often	Very Often	Specific comments, observations, and examples should be provided whenever possible.
VII. COORDINATION/MOTOR FUNCTION						
73. Has difficulty performing gross motor tasks (walking, sports, driving).						
74. Has difficulty performing fine motor tasks (writing, drawing).						
75. Confuses left-right.						
76. Has difficulty keeping balance.						
77. Has slow reaction time.						
78. Has limited endurance/stamina for motor activity.						
VIII. COMMUNICATION						
79. Has difficulty understanding words.						
80. Has difficulty learning new words.						
81. Does not respond appropriately to information presented verbally (conversation, directions).						

82. Has difficulty communicating on the phone.
83. Fails to form speech sounds correctly.
84. Substitutes one sound for another.
85. Makes sound omissions.
86. Substitutes words inappropriately.
87. Has word-finding difficulties.
88. Uses short, simple sentences.
89. Has difficulty expressing ideas clearly.

IX. READING SKILLS/COMPREHENSION

90. Has lack of phonemic awareness (i.e., words that are composed of sounds).
91. Reverses letters (i.e., b for d or *saw* for *was*).
92. Has difficulty reading signs in the environment.
93. Has difficulty reading newspapers.
94. Has difficulty reading job applications.
95. Has difficulty reading aloud.
96. Reading comprehension is below expected level.

X. WRITING/SPELLING

97. Has difficulty copying.
98. Has difficulty writing legibly.

(Continues)

Figure 3.5. Continued.

©1998 by PRO-ED, Inc.

Strengths and Limitations Inventory: School Version (Continued)

Please check each item based on your personal interview, knowledge and/or observation.	No Opportunity to Observe	Never	Sometimes	Often	Very Often	Specific comments, observations, and examples should be provided whenever possible.
99. Makes multiple spelling errors.						
100. Has difficulty communicating through writing.						
101. Has difficulty with paragraph organization.						
102. Makes errors in grammar or punctuation.						
103. Writing skills are below expected level.						
XI. MATH CALCULATION/APPLICATION						
104. Reverses numbers.						
105. Confuses math symbols.						
106. Has difficulty performing math calculations.						
107. Has difficulty performing math word problems.						
108. Has difficulty managing money.						
109. Has difficulty balancing checkbook.						
110. Math skills are below expected level.						

SUMMARY/INTERVENTION PLAN

Identified Strengths (Identify characteristics checked as never or seldom occurring. List those that may facilitate classroom success or be used in developing an appropriate accommodation or remediation strategy.)

Areas of Concern

(Review characteristics checked as often or very often occurring. These should be targeted as potential classroom limitations that may require remediation or a reasonable accommodation. Prioritize concerns if there are too many to be addressed simultaneously.)

Intervention: Accommodations and/or Remediation Techniques

(For suggestions specific to each characteristic, refer to the *Guide to Classroom Intervention* in Appendix A.)

Figure 3.5. Continued.

Table 3.1
Frequently Used Rating Scales Grouped by Purpose

Purpose	Rating Scales	Authors
ADHD-related symptoms	ADHD Rating Scale, for parents and teachers	DuPaul (1991)
	Attention-Deficit/Hyperactivity Disorder Test (ADHDT)	Gilliam (1995)
Home situations	Home Situations Questionnaire	Barkley & Edelbrock (1987), revised by DuPaul (1992)
School situations	Attention Deficit Disorders Evaluation Scale, teacher and parent versions	McCarney (1989)
	Schools Situations Questionnaires	Barkley & Edelbrock (1987), revised by DuPaul (1992)
	ADD-H Comprehensive Teacher Rating Scale (ACTeRS)	Ullmann, Sleator, Sprague (1984)
Multidimensional	Child Behavior Checklist (CBCL), teacher and parent forms	Achenbach (1991)
	Conners' Parent Rating Scales	Conners (1989)
	Conners' Teacher Rating Scales	Conners (1989)
	Revised Behavior Problem Checklist, for parents and teachers	Quay & Peterson (1983)
	Yale Children's Inventory	Shaywitz, Schnell, Shaywitz, & Towle (1986)
	Strengths and Limitations Inventory: School Version	Dowdy (1996)

- determining any contraindication to medication and establishing a baseline that can be used as a comparison when and if medication is administered

A medical examination may not be required in the school's diagnostic procedures for identifying ADHD. If the diagnostic team determines that a medical exam is indicated, the school may be required to pay for it. According to federal law, a medical examination *required* to assist the team in making a school-related decision is considered a "related service" and school systems must provide it (Worthington, Patterson, Elliott, & Linkous, 1993).

Follow-up Meeting of the Child-Study Team

When data have been collected from the multiple sources and settings described above, the child-study team should meet for eligibility determination.

At this second meeting of the child-study team, the data are presented by the person trained to identify ADHD. At this time the diagnostic questions posed earlier in the chapter should be answered if adequate data has been gathered. The following *DSM–IV* criteria should be considered:

- Six or more of the nine characteristics of ADHD-inattention and/or six or more of the nine symptoms of hyperactivity-impulsivity should be documented as present for longer than six months.

- The behaviors observed should be considered maladaptive and developmentally inconsistent.

- The symptoms should have been observed since or before age seven.

- The limitations from the characteristics should be observed in two or more settings (e.g., home and school or work).

- The characteristics are not considered solely the result of schizophrenia, pervasive developmental disorder, or other psychotic disorder, and they are not better attributed to the presence of another mental disorder such as anxiety disorder or mood disorder.

These criteria may be addressed through a thorough review of the data collected during the assessment process. Table 3.2 details the relationship between various assessment tools described and the *DSM–IV* criteria.

The child-study team should look for consistency across informants and the presence of attention-deficit symptoms across assessment instruments to validate the existence of ADHD. When the presence of the ADHD symptoms has been documented, the team should deter-

Table 3.2
School Assessment Procedures That
Can Be Used to Address *DSM–IV* Criteria

DSM–IV Criteria	Assessment Procedure
1. Documentation of characteristics of ADHD: inattention, hyperactivity, impulsivity	Observations Interviews School record review Rating scales IQ and academic assessment
2. Six months' persistence of maladaptive symptoms	Interviews School records
3. Behaviors inconsistent w/developmental level	Intellectual assessment Peer comparison-observation
4. Some symptoms present before age 7	School records Interviews Observations
5. Impairment present in two or more settings	Interviews Observations Rating scales School records
6. Evidence of impairment in academic, social, or occupational functioning	Observations Interviews School records Rating scales
7. Symptoms not result of another mental disorder, schizophrenia, pervasive developmental or other psychotic disorder	Observations Rating scales Intellectual assessment Medical exam

mine if there is an adverse effect on school performance and if specialized services are needed. Montague, McKinney, and Hocutt (1994) cite the following questions developed by the Professional Group on Attention and Related Disorders (PGARD) to guide the team in determining educational need:

1. Do the ADHD symptoms hinder learning by negatively affecting the child's ability to listen, follow directions, plan, organize, or complete academic tasks that require reading, math, writing, or spelling?

2. Are inattentive behaviors the result of cultural or language differences, socioeconomic disadvantage, or lack of exposure to education?

3. Are the inattentive behaviors evidence of stressful family functioning (e.g., divorce or death), abuse, frustration from unattainable academic goals, emotional or physical disorders (e.g., depression or epilepsy)?

Educational need requiring special services may be indicated if question one is answered affirmatively and questions two and three answered negatively. If the data supports the presence of ADHD, the following information and recommendations may be made available to the parents:

- an overview of their right to disagree with the results of the assessment, their right to obtain an outside evaluation, and their right to due process

- the names of parent groups that offer support and information regarding ADHD

- the educational services available to their child under the provisions of Section 504 and a brief overview of strategies that may be considered at the next child-study team meeting for implementation in the classroom

- a video developed by widely respected professionals explaining ADHD (Burnley, 1993)

- parent training in behavior management skills (The school counselor may need to discuss ADHD more fully with the parents, including various coping skills and the impact of ADHD on the parent-child interaction [Burnley, 1993].)

- information regarding stimulant medication, possible side effects, and the school's role in administering and monitoring medication, if the parents choose to follow up with a visit to a physician (Burnley, 1993)

Step 3: Collaborative Meeting for Strategy Development

The information relayed to parents in the eligibility determination meeting can evoke intense emotions and can be very overwhelming. It is important to hold the next meeting, for intervention strategy development, at least one week after the eligibility meeting. This gives the parents and the professional members of the team time to process the information and identify questions that have emerged after the meeting. Professionals and parents should agree to discuss the results of the assessment with the student to allay fears and impart information regarding his or her unique strengths and weaknesses. Students who are of middle-school age may wish to participate in the child-study team planning meetings (Fell & Pierce, 1995).

Although Section 504 does not require an extensive individualized educational plan (IEP) as mandated by IDEA, a plan is required. This is sometimes referred to as a Student Accommodation Plan, an Individual Accommodation Plan, or a 504 Plan. The plan should be developed by a committee that includes parents, professionals, and the student. Areas of weakness and strength should be reviewed at the planning meeting. Strengths are an important consideration in developing successful accommodations. The areas of concern causing significant limitations in learning should be targeted for developing a goal for improvement. The SLI (Figure 3.5) includes a summary section that can provide a framework for the process of developing an intervention plan.

A goal or plan of action may not be necessary for every weakness. The committee should agree on the least amount of modification, accommodation, and remediation needed to promote success in learning and social development. An extensive list of goals and action plans may create dependency and may not be beneficial to the student's transition to independent living and work. Additional goals and interventions can easily be added if necessary.

The team may need to address some of the following areas in developing a personalized education plan. A discussion of each of these will be found in the chapters that follow.

1. managing the classroom environment
   - group management
   - physical management
   - behavior management
   - modifications for individual characteristics

2. instructional accommodations
   - planning
   - grouping
   - material modification
   - teaching techniques
   - homework
   - testing

3. developing student-regulated strategies
   - self-management
   - learning strategies
   - study and organizational tactics
   - social skills
   - use of medication
   - parent role
   - teacher/school responsibility

Since no format has been mandated or recommended by the federal government, the method of compliance and the format for written plans vary from district to district. Three examples of formats that are being used currently are included in Figures 3.6 to 3.8.

Step 4: Follow-up and Progress Review

According to Burnley (1993), the teacher and counselor should meet weekly during the first month of the intervention plan to determine if it is successful. If some behaviors are not showing improvement after

---

Personalized Education Plan

Student_____ Grade _____

Parents _____ Phone _____

Address _____

Date_____ Review Date _____

Student's Strengths	Student's Weaknesses

Goal 1:

Plan of Action   Person Responsible

Goal 2:

Plan of Action   Person Responsible

(Continues)

Figure 3.6. Personalized education plan. *Note.* Developed by B. D. Mayer and J. U. Turner, 1993, unpublished manuscript adopted by the Hoover City School System, Birmingham, Alabama. Reprinted with permission.

Personalized Education Plan

Goal 3:

      Plan of Action   Person Responsible

Goal 4:

      Plan of Action   Person Responsible

504 Committee Member Signatures   **Position**

_____   Parent

_____   Principal/Assistant

_____   Learning Support Teacher

_____   Teacher

_____   _____

_____   _____

_____   _____

Figure 3.6. Continued.

General Education Accommodation Plan

Name: _Joshua Green_

Date: _6/5/95_

School/Grade: _Platte Valley Elementary, 3rd_

Teacher: _Myrna Mae (lead teacher)_

Participants in Development of Accommodation Plan

Mr. and Mrs. Walter Green / _Julie Hartson_ / _Myrna Mae, Teacher_ / _Arlo Wachal, Teacher_
parent(s)/guardian(s)　　principal　　teacher(s)

Joel Schaeffer, Counselor　　_Violette Schelldorf, Nurse_

Building Person Responsible for Monitoring Plan: _Joel Schaeffer, Counselor_　Follow-up Date: _6/5/96_

Currently on Medication ☒ Yes ☐ No　Physician _Eveard Ewing, M.D._　Type _Ritalin_　Dosage _15 mg. twice daily_

Area of Concern	Intervention of Teaching Strategies	Person Responsible for Accommodation
1. Assignment Completion	1. Daily assignment sheet sent home with Josh	Myrna Mae Parents will initial daily, and Josh will return the form
	2. Contract system initiated for assignment completion in math and social studies	Myrna Mae, Arlo Wachal
2. Behavior/Distractibility	1. Preferential seating—study carrel or near teacher, as needed	Myrna Mae, Arlo Wachal
	2. Daily behavior card sent home with Josh	Parents will initial daily, and Josh will return the form

3. Consistency of Medication	1. Medication to be administered in private by school nurse daily at noon	Violette Schelldorf

Comments:

Josh will remain in the general education classroom with the accommodations noted above.

Parental Authorization for 504 Plan

I agree with the accommodations described in this 504 plan.	Parent Signature	I do not agree with the accommodations described in this 504 plan. I understand I have the right to appeal.

Figure 3.7. General education accommodation plan—example. (Information and names are fictional.) *Note.* From "Section 504 Accommodation Plans," by G. Conderman and A. Katsiyannis, 1995, *Intervention in School and Clinic, 31*(1), p. 44. Copyright 1995 by PRO-ED, Inc. Reprinted with permission.

Student Accommodation Plan

Name: _____ Date of Meeting: _____

Date of Birth: _____ School: _____ Grade: _____

1. Describe the nature of the concern:

2. Describe the basis for the determination of disability (if any):

3. Describe how the disability affects a major life activity:

4. Describe the reasonable accommodations that are necessary:

5. Review/reassessment date (must be completed):

6. Participants (name and title):

cc: Student's Cumulative File

Figure 3.8. Sample Section 504 plan. *Note.* From Maryland Learning Disabilities Association (1995) *Summer Newsletter.* Copyright 1995 by Maryland Learning Disabilities Association. Reprinted with permission.

a month, adjustments will need to be made. If a reinforcement system was implemented, it may be necessary to change the reinforcer or to consider the option of frequently changing reinforcers, and novel consequences will need to be identified more often. If the student was put on a self-management plan, it may be determined that this is too large a step. A teacher-directed reinforcement system may be necessary initially with a more systematic transition to self-management.

One of the best ways to monitor the success of the intervention plan over time is to continue observation techniques such as recording behavior in logs (refer to Figure 3.2) and periodically repeating the more structured observation technique, TOAD, described earlier. The initial observations can serve as a baseline to compare behavior observed following intervention. Taking similar data on randomly selected normal peers allows important comparisons.

In-class observation and comparison are important measures of how the student with ADHD is coping in the real world. Again, caution must be used when evaluating the results of an outside observer entering the environment. The teacher should be asked to validate the behavior as typical for that setting. Parents and the children themselves should also be consulted regarding their evaluation of the success of the intervention plan.

Final Thoughts

Even if the plan is currently judged to be effective, the assessment and follow-up will not be over. As the environment, people, and activities change, new plans must be created and evaluated. New teams will be formed at each grade level. As students become efficient learners and demonstrate better social skills under one level of control, a new, less restrictive intervention plan must be designed and implemented. Evaluation and change should occur until the student is capable of self-regulated behavior and is able to be a self-advocate when the need arises.

CHAPTER 4

Managing the Classroom Environment

S tudents with ADHD often represent major challenges for teachers, especially general classroom teachers not used to teaching students who display the characteristics of this group. Adding to this challenge is the fact that many regular classroom teachers have not been trained in how to deal with students with ADHD. Most teacher education programs, especially those that train teachers for general elementary classrooms or secondary classrooms, only include a minimal amount of information on teaching students with these kinds of problems.

One or two students with ADHD can easily disrupt an entire room if their behaviors are not managed properly. Therefore, teachers must understand basic classroom management techniques, which include managing all aspects of the classroom environment.

Several assumptions related to classroom management should be considered when preparing to deal with students with ADHD (Duke & Meckel, 1984). First, *classroom management is an integral part of teaching.* Without adequate classroom management, teaching cannot be effective, especially when students with ADHD are in the classroom. The second assumption is that *teachers can be trained to handle behavior problems effectively.* Classroom management techniques are not magical, and teachers are not born with classroom management skills. Rather, classroom management techniques are a compilation of methods that can be effective in managing environments to enhance the learning of all students. The third assumption is that *teachers are in the best position to determine how they most effectively can manage their classrooms.* The specific way teachers manage their classrooms is unique to each teacher. A method that works for one teacher may not work for another. Also, district supervisory personnel cannot dictate effective classroom management techniques. Teachers must be given flexibility in their use of classroom management techniques with all students, including those with ADHD.

The fourth assumption dealing with classroom management is that *teachers often are so busy reacting to day-to-day problems that they fail to reflect on the purposes of classroom management.* Obviously, teachers often get caught up in surviving crises, which can easily occur when working with students with ADHD. *Reacting* to situations rather than having a system for *managing* situations should be avoided.

The final assumption is that *teaching is one of the most important, challenging, and frustrating occupations in contemporary society.* This assumption is obvious for most of us. Teaching is critical in our society since the educational system is expected to prepare children for an increasingly changing world. And teaching is obviously frustrating, particularly when students with ADHD are present. Classroom management techniques can help teachers and other school personnel reduce the frustration associated with teaching and facilitate learning for all students in a classroom.

Classroom management does not mean behavior modification, assertive discipline, or any other single method of controlling behaviors in the classroom. Rather, classroom management is the combination of techniques that result in an orderly classroom environment in which academic and social growth can occur. Classroom management, therefore, includes a variety of techniques, including group management, physical management, and behavior management. Good classroom management can result in successful educational programs for all students, including those with ADHD.

Group Management

Teachers often rely on group-management techniques to assist in controlling behaviors of individual students with ADHD. Group-management techniques are ways teachers manage all members of a classroom. These include establishing classroom rules and consequences, arranging the classroom schedule, grouping students, and offering special class incentives (Smith, Polloway, Patton, & Dowdy, 1995). When used effectively, these techniques help manage the behaviors of all students, including those with ADHD.

Classroom Rules and Consequences

A very good method for managing classroom behaviors is to establish rules for the entire classroom. Students, including those with ADHD, need to know what is expected of them and what the consequences will be if the rules are not observed. It is a simple fact that most students do best when they know what is expected of them and the likely consequences for not meeting those expectations (Polloway & Patton, 1993). There are several ways teachers can develop rules. First, they can decide on their rules before students arrive in the classroom. When deciding on rules, teachers should consider the most important classroom behaviors that will or will not be allowed. Rules should not be elaborate but should simply reflect important dos and don'ts. Another way of choosing rules is to allow students to help develop them. Having students help develop classroom rules often gives them a sense of ownership and may result in better results than when students are not involved. When getting students involved in making rules, teachers must be able to insert the rule or rules they think are important. Teachers could always start off by saying, "We are going to decide on some rules for the classroom. I will be able to add one or two rules of my own, but you should start thinking about what rules you want." This kind of beginning statement enables teachers to add rules that need to be listed but that are not developed by students.

When making rules for the classroom, teachers need to remember the following guidelines (Smith et al., 1995):

1. Rules should be stated positively when at all possible. For example, a rule of "Stay in your seat" is better than one that says "Do not get out of your seat."

2. Rules should be stated simply so all children are able to understand them. If students are unable to read, rules can be depicted with drawings.

3. The number of rules should be kept to a manageable number, probably no more than five or six.

4. Rules should be posted conspicuously, maybe even in more than one location in the room. Using poster board and color markers helps make rules visible.

5. At the beginning of the school year, teachers should have their class say the rules every day, maybe even more than once each day in the beginning. If, during the year, rules begin to be ignored, teachers may want to reinstitute this method of reminding everyone of the rules.

6. Rules should be enforceable. While it might be nice if a rule said not to talk to a "neighbor," it is unlikely that that rule would be enforced on a routine basis. Having rules that are enforced sometimes but not always will only confuse students.

7. Students who abide by the rules should be positively reinforced. Simply using rules to punish students who break them does not result in good use of rules to manage behaviors.

An example of classroom rules can be found in Figure 4.1.

Rules should be posted in places that are easily observable. An attractive display of the rules will help focus students' attention. Once developed, teachers should go over the rules with all students regularly, especially in the beginning of a school year, to reinforce the notion that the rules are important and to ensure that all students understand them. At all times, teachers should be consistent in applying the rules in the classroom. This is the most important aspect of classroom rules. When not applied consistently, classroom rules can become a barrier to classroom management because students do not know when they will or will not be enforced. It is very important that attention to classroom rules does not occur only when rules are broken; teachers should also praise students for following rules. Having rules that are acknowledged only when they are broken, which is likely followed by negative consequences, can easily create a negative classroom atmosphere. Teachers must provide positive reinforcements to students when rules are followed.

Finally, teachers should communicate classroom rules to parents. Parents need to understand rules and how consequences will be applied if rules are broken. Informing parents about rules and consequences will increase the support teachers get from home. One good way to do this is to send rules home at the beginning of the year and ask parents to discuss the rules with their children. Following this discussion, both parent and child should sign the rules and return them to the teacher.

Examples of Classroom Rules

1. Stay in your seat.

2. Keep your hands to yourself.

3. Take turns talking.

4. Raise your hand before talking out.

5. Walk in the school instead of running.

Figure 4.1. Examples of classroom rules.

Classroom Schedule

Time management is a very important component of classroom management. The classroom schedule sets the tone for the entire school day. If the schedule is structured to the degree that students do not have a lot of free time, it is less likely that students with attention problems will display inappropriate behaviors. Free time can be a part of the schedule, but it also should be structured to some degree. Free time without any structure can be very difficult for students with ADHD to manage. Gallagher (1979) notes some specific considerations for teachers when developing daily schedules. These include:

- Provide students with a daily schedule.

- Alternate tasks that are high probability with those that are low probability.

- Always schedule work that can be completed by the end of the day or period.

- Plan for some flexible time.

- Always require students to complete a task before moving to other tasks.

- Have ways to remind students about their time (how much has elapsed and how much remains on a task).

- Do not assign additional work for students who finish their work early.

- Always plan ahead, anticipating what students will need.

- Establish expectations for students in advance and do not introduce unexpected requirements after beginning an activity.

- Provide feedback to students so they will know how they are doing.

- Provide positive feedback when at all possible, avoiding indicators of failure.

Most teachers begin their day with a set routine. This might include a variety of activities, including listening to and singing the national anthem, saying the Pledge of Allegiance, recognizing birthdays, collecting lunch money, discussing the day of the month, and talking about any special events that are coming up (Polloway & Patton, 1997). Some teachers, even in lower elementary grades, begin their days with quiet reading time. Students know to get a book and sit quietly at their desks and read, or at least look at pictures. Beginning with several short activities is generally a good way to get the day started because it helps students pay attention to an activity, especially when they are just getting started in the day (Lewis & Doorlag, 1995). It helps them get into "school gear."

The beginning part of each day is important for all students but especially for those with ADHD. The beginning activities should set the stage for a calm, orderly day with specific expectations by the teacher. Getting off to a good start will significantly improve the chance that students will have a good day. Just the opposite is more likely to occur when students begin the day in a disruptive manner.

Teachers should establish schedules that reflect the entire day's activities. Although these schedules may be altered from time to time, they should provide the general sequence of activities for each day. Students with ADHD like to know what's coming. They need to be able to understand that reading is over at 10:30, then spelling, then lunch, then recess. This kind of structured day helps students with ADHD keep "tuned in" to classroom activities.

Teachers should arrange a variety of activities that will bring closure to the day's work, as well as provide reminders for students if they need to do something before the next day. Closing activities might include such things as straightening up desks, relocating materials to their appropriate places, and lining up for dismissal. Closing activity time presents an excellent opportunity for teachers to provide rewards for students who have displayed appropriate behaviors during the day. Many teachers do this with hand stamps that they use as students exit the classroom.

There is no single classroom schedule appropriate for all classrooms, even for all classrooms at the same grade level. Classroom schedules will vary because of external factors, such as when assemblies and lunch are scheduled, and internal factors, such as the teacher's preference for when to teach certain subjects. Regardless of differences, teachers should understand the importance of schedules, especially as they relate to routines that all students can learn to expect. Figure 4.2 depicts a sample schedule for a second-grade class.

Sample Daily Schedule for Second-Grade Classroom

8:00–8:15	Silent reading
8:15–8:30	Anthem, pledge, and announcements
8:30–9:15	Group reading
9:15–10:00	Math activities
10:00–10:55	Language arts
10:55–11:05	Restroom/prepare for lunch
11:05–11:35	Lunch
11:35–12:00	Recess
12:00–12:45	Story time/rest time
12:45–1:30	Journal writing
1:30–2:15	Music/PE/art (alternates days)
2:15–2:30	Complete all work/clean up areas
2:30–2:45	Announcements/prepare to go home

Figure 4.2. Sample daily schedule for second-grade classroom.

Grouping Students

The way students are grouped may have an impact on the manage-ability of the classroom. Groups will vary from the entire class to small groups, to one-on-one or two-person groups. The size of the group will generally be determined by the nature of the activity. In grouping students, teachers must keep two things in mind: the desired size of the group, and the type of group (Lewis, & Doorlag, 1995). The teacher may prefer small groups of four to seven students to work on a par-ticular project to facilitate the accomplishment of a group goal, or groups of only two or three students. The groups may be skill specific, that is groups composed of students who are working on the same skill level, or they may be grouped along other lines, such as by name, by gender, or by self-selection. Allowing students to self-group will frequently result in students who display behavior problems being together. This might be due to other students not wanting those with behavior problems in their group, or because students who seemingly get into trouble a great deal form their own bond and group. Regardless of the reason, teachers will probably not want students who display behavior problems to always be together. Therefore, teacher-controlled grouping, at least in many activities, may be war-ranted.

Other than simply not wanting several students together who may likely cause problems, there are numerous positive reasons for group-ing students who have difficulty managing their behavior with stu-dents who do not have that problem:

- Students who do not have behavior problems are positive role models for other students.

- Students who display behavior problems may be subjected to peer pressure to abide by classroom rules.

- Students with behavior problems may become friends with stu-dents who do not display or tolerate such problems and want to fit in with those children.

Some students have a very difficult time interacting positively with their peers and may actually need one-to-one instruction as opposed to group instruction. In determining if a student requires one-to-one instruction, Polloway and Patton (1993) suggest that teachers consider the effectiveness of using one-to-one instruction, the efficiency of using that model, and the social benefits that the student may be missing in a one-to-one instructional format. For the most part, students with ADHD need to interact with their peers because of their need to secure social competence; however, there may be some instances in which students, at least from time to time, need a one-to-one format in order to achieve and in order to allow their peers to achieve.

Special Classroom Incentives

Teachers can use classroom incentives to help with behavior management in their classrooms. Special classroom incentives are a way of applying classroom management techniques to a class as a whole. When using classroom incentives, teachers take advantage of all students in the classroom helping with classroom management, primarily through the use of peer pressure and peer support. In this system, students become their own "managers" of the classroom environment. One frequently used technique for implementing this method is for teachers to place a marble in a large jar every time students display appropriate behaviors. When the jar is filled, the class receives an award, such as a popcorn party, pizza party, or picnic on the school grounds. Another classroom incentive method is to put a puzzle together, one piece at a time, when the teacher recognizes the entire class for appropriate behaviors. Once the puzzle is complete, the class receives some reward. Classroom incentives can be a powerful tool in helping manage the entire classroom environment. Their use enables teachers to take advantage of classroom peers to help achieve classroom management goals.

Physical Management

Managing the physical environment of the classroom often has an impact on the behavior of all students, including those with ADHD. The physical environment includes such things as the physical dimensions and arrangement of the classroom, the location of materials, the classroom decor, the movement style of the teacher, and the traffic patterns of the students, as well as other environmental considerations.

Physical Dimensions and Arrangement of the Classroom

Students with ADHD often react to the physical aspects of the class-room, including the classroom dimensions and the way the classroom is arranged. Lewis and Doorlag (1995) state that the physical environment, the classroom, has a significant influence on nonacademic activities of students. This definitely includes the behavior of students. For example, if students are cramped together, there will be more opportunities for touching, pinching, and physically aggravating each other than if they have ample personal space. Unless the classroom is too small to accommodate the number of students assigned, teachers can arrange desks to provide students with this personal "space." This should greatly limit opportunities for unwanted physical and verbal interactions that might be inappropriate and disruptive.

Physical Dimensions

The size of the classroom is an important consideration for classroom management. Spaces that are too small are very difficult to arrange in a way that lessens the likelihood of behavior problems. When students are in very close proximity with each other, opportunities for physical aggravation are high. Students simply have a hard time keeping their hands off each other, especially those students who have problems with attention and hyperactivity.

Limited space also makes it difficult for teachers to use learning and interest centers, which provide excellent opportunities for students to work in small groups or individually on projects that are interesting and fun, just the kinds of things that help keep students with ADHD on track. Classrooms that are too small also impact on the movement style of teachers and the traffic patterns of students, two areas that can make a big difference for students with ADHD. Teachers should lobby for sufficient space to provide for flexibility in desk arrangements, traffic patterns, and learning and interest centers.

Arrangement of Desks

The traditional method of arranging desks in classrooms has been row by row. In this arrangement, students sit behind each other in several rows. While this arrangement of desks might work well for some classes, there are some disadvantages, as:

- students are tempted to interfere with students who have their backs to them;

- students, other than the ones sitting near the front, are difficult to observe by the teacher;

- students in the rear have difficulty seeing the front of the room, including the teacher when something is being explained on the board.

These problems are often worse when the classroom includes a student with ADHD, but they can be overcome with a simple rearrangement of the classroom.

Several arrangements—including grouping desks in small clusters or grouping desks in large circles—might be tried by teachers to eliminate some of the problem areas that encourage students to act inappropriately. The following summarizes some advantages and disadvantages of different grouping arrangements.

Room Arrangement	Advantages/Disadvantages
Vertical rows	• create an orderly environment
	• make it difficult for teacher to see students in the back
	• create opportunities for students to physically interact with each other
	• make it difficult for students in the back to see or hear teacher
Large group circle	• allows teacher to see all students easily
	• allows students to see teacher easily
	• limits opportunities for physical interactions among students
	• facilitates discussion
	• provides alternative to traditional row-by-row seating

(Continues on next page)

Small clusters	• require teachers to move about the room
	• facilitate student interactions
	• make it difficult for teachers to see all students at all times
	• restrict total group discussion
	• provide alternative to traditional row-by-row seating

Instructional activities in the classroom are directly affected by classroom arrangements. For example, classrooms need ample space for students to work in a variety of groupings. The space should be arranged to enable students to work independently, as well as in small groups and large groups. Ample storage space for materials is also needed, and classroom space needs to be arranged functionally to ensure that all of the different activities that occur routinely can be accomplished within the space available.

In addition to the physical arrangement of the classroom, several other factors related to classroom dimensions and arrangement will have an impact on classroom management. These include the use of study carrels, interest centers, and bulletin boards (Polloway & Patton, 1997). Table 4.1 describes each of these.

Location of Materials

Teachers frequently have materials stored or displayed in the classroom, especially teachers in elementary classrooms. While materials might not be distracting to some students, students with ADHD may not be able to "ignore" the presence of these objects. When materials become a major distraction, teachers may need to store them out of the sight of students. Closets with doors are the best solution. Another solution is to cover shelves with curtains that act as doors. Teachers also may use sturdy boxes that can be closed. The boxes can be placed on shelves, or even under furniture, to reduce temptation. Such boxes can be obtained with limited or no cost to the teacher.

Classroom Decor

Although teachers may like to have "stuff" all over their rooms, this could prove to be very distracting for students with ADHD. While it

Table 4.1
Other Factors Related to Classroom Management

Factor	Impact on Management
Study Carrels	• Can be used to isolate individual students for time-out purposes
	• Can be used to isolate individual students to reduce external stimuli, both auditory and visual
	• Can facilitate individual student's ability to attend to learning tasks
	• Can be used as a positive reinforcer for some students
Interest Centers	• Can be used for small-group instructional activities
	• Can provide incentives for students and be used as positive reinforcers
	• Can promote teamwork with other students
	• Can provide opportunities for teachers to group students based on various criteria
Bulletin Boards	• May be distracting if too "busy"
	• May be used as a reinforcer by letting students design them and/or put them up
	• May be used as a location for posting classroom rules and other important information
	• May be used as a location for posting positive reinforcement information

is not recommended to make classrooms sterile and colorless, teachers should consider the potential distraction of certain visual displays. It is recommended that teachers use a few bulletin boards and displays that are colorful but not overwhelming.

In addition to visual displays, teachers should be aware of clutter. Stacks of papers, boxes, materials, and other items may be very distracting to students. Teachers should have a method of physically organizing their papers and materials to avoid stacks of things that can prove detrimental to students, especially those with ADHD. Storing materials in file cabinets is the best method of dealing with these materials.

Still another factor related to classroom decor is the emotional environment that is created in the classroom. Classrooms can be described as *cold, busy, warm,* or *secure.* For example, a classroom with tile floors, few windows, and bare bulletin boards might be classified as cold, whereas a room with carpet, colorful bulletin boards, and bright windows might be considered warm. The *feelings* that come from various physical environments may affect children's moods and behaviors and should be considered by teachers when developing strategies for working with students with ADHD.

Movement Style of the Teacher

The movement style of teachers may have an impact on managing the behaviors of students with ADHD. Some teachers like to sit at their desks and direct most learning activities from that place in the room. Many students, however, need the teacher to be in close proximity, at least occasionally, to help them control their attention and behaviors. Teachers should therefore move about the room when involved in instructional activities. The mere physical presence of a teacher near a student is frequently sufficient to help the student focus on the learning activity and reduce inappropriate behaviors.

When the teacher is in another part of the classroom and a student or group of students begins acting inappropriately, a first step for the teacher should always be to move closer to the disruptive students. Often this increase in proximity is all that is necessary to restore appropriate behavior. The teacher is thus able to reduce classroom distractions, caused by the disruptive students, without implementing a strategy that in itself is distracting. The same approach is effective in helping students attend to specific learning activities.

Traffic Patterns of Students

The traffic patterns of students also can have an impact on students with ADHD. If the predominant traffic pattern used by most students results in numerous opportunities for students to physically interact with each other, students with ADHD may have a difficult time focusing on learning tasks and not bothering other students. In classrooms with such traffic patterns, teachers may want to have students with

ADHD seated outside the normal traffic flow. This will lessen their chances of being frequently distracted by students walking by, thus helping them attend to specific tasks and abide by classroom rules more easily.

Behavior Management

Behavior management is the application of behavioral theory to classroom situations (Jones & Jones, 1995). It is frequently used in classrooms and by parents to manage children's behaviors. Behavior management is one of the most effective methods of dealing with students with ADHD. With behavior-management techniques, teachers can help students stay on task, as well as control their physical behaviors. Behavior management can be defined as the application of behaviorism to classroom and learning environments (Smith et al., 1995). Behavior management focuses on maintaining or increasing a child's appropriate behaviors, such as staying in his or her seat and attending to a learning task, as well as decreasing inappropriate behaviors, such as being off-task or getting out of his or her seat.

Increasing Appropriate Behaviors

The most effective means of behavior management is the maintenance or increase of appropriate behaviors (Jones & Jones, 1995). Students with ADHD who are attending to an appropriate teaming activity, or who are following classroom rules, should be positively reinforced. Too often, however, teachers ignore appropriate behaviors and call attention only to those behaviors that are inappropriate, such as not paying attention or aggravating other students. By maintaining or increasing appropriate behaviors, inappropriate behaviors are less likely to occur in the first place. The primary method for maintaining and increasing appropriate behaviors is through the use of positive reinforcement (Smith, Finn, & Dowdy, 1993).

Principles of Positive Reinforcement

Positive reinforcement is a simple concept that has been proven to be extremely effective in managing classrooms and the behaviors of individual students (Jones & Jones, 1995; Smith et al., 1995). Positive reinforcement is based on the premise that students (and adults) do things that result in rewards. Adults work for several reasons. One is that they enjoy their work and that is rewarding; however, a second reason is that they receive money for their efforts. In this example, both the intrinsic enjoyment of working and the tangible reward, money, motivate the person to work. Both serve as positive reinforcers.

Positive reinforcement works the same way with students. Students will be more likely to tackle difficult challenges if their efforts result in rewards. Good grades, words of encouragement, and hugs may be sufficient rewards for some students. For others, the rewards may need to be more concrete, such as candy, a toy, or free time. Regardless of the type of reward, the theory is the same: people are more likely to do something again if after the first time they do it, something good happens to them. This approach can help students with ADHD pay attention to appropriate learning activities.

Positive Reinforcers

A critical component of positive reinforcement is the positive reinforcers that are used. Positive reinforcers are the rewards that are given to a person after successful completion of a task (Smith et al., 1995). A variety of different things and events can be used as positive reinforcers. Some of the more commonly used items and activities include:

- candy and other edibles
- toys
- clothes
- perfume
- free time
- time to listen to music
- opportunities to do things for the teacher
- time in the gym
- being read a story
- having lunch with the teacher
- going to a movie
- praise
- hugs

Of course, a positive reinforcer that works for one student may not work for another. If the person receiving the reward does not consider it rewarding, then the process will fail (Jones & Jones, 1995). For example, giving a student an ice cream cone after he has successfully completed a worksheet will not increase the likelihood that he will complete the next worksheet if he does not like ice cream. Therefore, it is critical that students be involved in selecting the positive reinforcers that are used. One way of doing this is to have students complete a reward survey. Figure 4.3 presents one example of such a survey.

Positive Reinforcement Programs

Positive reinforcement is a simple process that works well with most people, adults and students. Still, without a systematic method of implementing it in a school setting, the process may not be effective, or at least not as effective as it could be. There are several ways that teachers have successfully implemented positive reinforcement theory into their classrooms. These include the Premack principle, contingency contracting, and token economies.

Reinforcer Menu

Put a 1 next to the thing(s) you most want or want to do
Put a 2 next to the thing(s) you want or want to do, but not most
Put a 3 next to the thing(s) you do not care if you do/get or not

_____ candy bar
_____ toy car
_____ doll
_____ marbles
_____ sticker
_____ lunch with the teacher
_____ extra time on the playground
_____ time on the computer
_____ time at the listening center with music
_____ helping in the principal's office
_____ being teacher's helper for a day
_____ no homework

Figure 4.3. Reinforcer menu.

Premack Principle. The Premack principle is the most basic concept that deals with consequences. "It is called 'grandma's law' because it is reminiscent of the traditional dinner table remark, 'If you eat your vegetables, then you can have your dessert'" (Polloway & Patton, 1993, p. 102). All teachers and parents have used the Premack principle to get children to do things they do not want to do. The principle is that by doing something you don't want to do, you get something you want. In classroom situations, the Premack principle is used regularly when teachers use rewards such as free time, snacks, or a party after students have completed their work.

The Premack principle is easily adapted for classroom applications. Teachers can require students to complete less desirable activities before the activities that students want to do. Also, teachers can require students to exhibit specific types of behaviors before they are allowed to do things they want to do. For example, students with ADHD who have difficulty staying in their seats and completing their work can be required to stay in their seats for at least twenty minutes and complete a specific assignment before they can go outside for recess.

Contingency Contracting. Developing formal contracts with students is an excellent method to encourage appropriate behaviors in students with ADHD. In contingency contracting, the teacher and the student develop a contract built around the student's behavior and the resulting consequence. The important components of the contract are *what the student will or will not do,* and *what the teacher will do in response* (Westling & Koorland, 1988). This approach often works well with students with ADHD who need a simple structure, such as a contract, to enable them to achieve success.

One advantage of contracts is that they can be fun to develop (Wood, 1984). Also, because they put into writing specific activities that the student will perform and the specific reward that the teacher will provide, there is limited opportunity for the student or teacher to misunderstand what is expected or what the reinforcement will be. Westling and Koorland (1988) suggest the following guidelines when using contingency contracting:

- determine the target behavior or activity
- determine appropriate reinforcers
- agree on an appropriate length of time

- write the contingency in clear, concise language
- sign the contract (both teacher and student)
- keep a record of the student's behavior
- provide agreed-to positive reinforcer if contract is fulfilled
- write a new contract based on the successful completion of the contract

A sample contract is provided in Figure 4.4.

Token Economies. Token economies are another excellent method of applying positive reinforcement to classroom situations with children with ADHD. In a token economy, students earn tokens that can be redeemed for more concrete reinforcers after a period of time. The tokens can be anything that represents a positive response from the teacher: poker chips, pennies, or even checkmarks. The system works by students collecting enough tokens to redeem them for something they want, such as a toy, free time, or an activity (Polloway & Patton, 1997).

Wood (1984) has identified eight steps necessary in implementing a token economy system:

1. Teacher identifies target behavior.
2. Teacher clearly identifies for the student the behavior that will earn tokens.
3. Teacher posts appropriate behavior on a chart or on student's desk.
4. Teacher and student select reinforcers to exchange for tokens.
5. Teacher explains rules of token system to student.
6. Teacher asks student to explain system.
7. Teacher initiates token system.
8. Teacher evaluates token system.

Token economies are a good way to implement positive reinforcement in school settings (Jones & Jones, 1995). They provide enough structure to ensure that both teachers and students understand the program, while being simple enough not to create confusion.

Contract

This agreement is between _____
(student)

and _____. The contract begins on _____
(teacher)

and continues until _____ .

The terms of this contract include the following:

The student will:

_____

_____

_____

_____

When these things are completed, the teacher will:

_____

_____

_____

_____

Student's Signature _____ Date _____

Teacher's Signature _____ Date _____

Figure 4.4. Sample of contingency contract.

Decreasing Inappropriate Behaviors

One of the important components of a behavior-management program is how to decrease inappropriate behaviors. For students with ADHD, inappropriate behaviors include not attending to learning tasks, inappropriate movement about the room, inappropriate verbalizations, and excessive motor movements such as foot or finger tapping. Teachers need ways to help students decrease such behaviors to create an environment that is conducive to learning for all students.

There are numerous ways teachers and parents can help a child decrease inappropriate behaviors. These include not reinforcing inappropriate behaviors, differential reinforcement of appropriate behaviors, proximity control, preventive cueing, and punishment. No one method is effective for all students. Rather, teachers need to have a repertoire of interventions that can be used.

Removing Reinforcement Through Planned Ignoring

Often students receive reinforcement when they display inappropriate behaviors. Simply getting the teacher's attention may be the goal of a student who behaves inappropriately. In such a case, calling attention to an inappropriate behavior may serve as a reinforcer for the student even if the attention received is negative. A teacher who ignores a student's display of inappropriate behavior is withholding reinforcement. This planned ignoring of students who display inappropriate behaviors requires a great deal of teacher patience. Usually, when teachers first implement a planned-ignoring strategy, the inappropriate behavior increases. However, in many instances, if the teacher can "wait out" this temporary increase, the behavior will eventually subside (Wood, 1984). Planned ignoring must be coupled with positive reinforcement when the student ceases the inappropriate behavior or is involved in appropriate behaviors. Without this component, planned ignoring will not be successful (Smith et al., 1995).

Of course, some behaviors simply cannot be ignored. Behaviors that create disruptions in the classroom and interfere with other students' learning may not be possible to ignore. Also, some behaviors may be dangerous to the student exhibiting the behavior or to other students. In these situations, teachers must intervene; planned ignoring is simply not an option.

Reinforcement of Competing Behaviors

One way of decreasing inappropriate behaviors that has been shown to be effective is to positively reinforce appropriate behaviors that might interfere with the inappropriate behaviors. For example, if a student is frequently out of his seat, a method of dealing with that behavior is to provide positive reinforcement to the student when he is seated. This behavior-reduction technique is more similar to positively reinforcing appropriate behaviors than to reducing inappropriate behaviors. However, the rationale is to reduce an inappropriate behavior by reinforcing something that competes with that behavior. Another example is reinforcing students with attention problems when they are attending to a learning task.

Proximity Control

Simple proximity control is often a good method for reducing inappropriate behaviors and helping students maintain their attention. Proximity control has to do with the physical location of the teacher. Often students will behave inappropriately, or will get off-task, when the teacher is not near them. By standing or sitting near a particular student, teachers may be able to continue with a lesson or activity without interruptions (Wood, 1984).

Preventive Cueing and Signal Interference

Making students who may be on the verge of an inappropriate behavior aware of their potential behavior may prevent the behavior from occurring. Similarly, if the inappropriate behavior has begun, giving the student a cue to stop that behavior may be effective. Teachers may use signals as simple as making eye contact, raising a hand or finger, flipping the light switch, or turning their back to reveal displeasure with a behavior that is occurring or is about to occur (Wood, 1984). Such preventive or interfering methods are often effective without being disruptive to the class activities.

Punishment

When all else fails, there is always punishment. For the most part, punishment is not as effective in reducing inappropriate behaviors for students with ADHD as the other methods that have been presented. However, there may be instances when punishment is the desired intervention by teachers. Punishment can be defined as applying unpleasant consequences to behaviors. Punishment includes such things as giving verbal reprimands, making students do extra work, restricting students' free time, making students stay after school, and reducing students' privileges, as well as the most controversial, corporal punishment (Smith et al., 1993). We all remember being punished for doing certain things, or not doing certain things, by either teachers or parents. Sometimes the punishment was effective, and sometimes it was not.

There are several key points regarding punishment that teachers and other school personnel should always consider. These include:

1. Teachers and other school personnel should use punishment only after other behavior management techniques have failed. Positive and preventive methods are always preferred over punishment.

2. Punishment is most effective when it is used in conjunction with positive reinforcement (Lewis & Doorlag, 1995).

3. Punishment should always fit the inappropriate behavior. Using severe punishment for behaviors that are not serious is very inappropriate. If punishment is used, it should always be related to the seriousness of the behavior.

4. If punishment is used, it should be used immediately after the behavior, not delayed for a period of time (Westling & Koorland, 1988).

5. Physical punishment should never be administered by someone who is angry or upset. Teachers need to be aware of their emotions to ensure that they are in control before they punish a student (Westling & Koorland, 1988).

6. Teachers should keep records of any punishment used. These records, in addition to ensuring an accurate reflection of events, may be used by teachers to determine the effectiveness of such intervention strategies (Westling & Koorland, 1988).

Using Time-Out Effectively. Often, teachers use time-out as punishment. Time-out can be defined as the withdrawal of positive reinforcement from a student. "Although techniques may differ, the concept generally entails preventing a student from receiving the positive reinforcement that otherwise would be available" (Polloway & Patton, 1993, p. 110). Time-out can take the form of planned ignoring (previously discussed); removal of a student from direct participation in the group, although the student can observe the group; or total removal of the student from the classroom. Removal of the student from the classroom is the most severe form of time-out and should be restricted for significant behavior problems.

Removing a student from the classroom is not something that should be taken lightly. It is considered a severe form of punishment. When this form of time-out is used, several considerations must be made (Westling & Koorland, 1988):

- Make sure the student is observable during the time-out.

- Use an area that is away from the major activities of the class and make sure there is a chair or carpeted floor in the area.

- Use time-out only for brief periods of time, generally five to ten minutes, and set a timer to remind the teacher and student when the time-out is over.

- Always inform the student why he is being placed in time-out at the onset of the time-out period.

- Allow the student to come out of time-out on his own when the timer goes off.

If the student does not want to come out of time-out, leave him in; do not force him to come out. Most states have specific rules and policies related to the use of time-out. Teachers and other school personnel should be aware of these rules and policies to ensure that their school is implementing them properly.

Modifications for Specific Characteristics

Group- and physical-management techniques may not always be effective with individual students with ADHD. For many of these students, teachers and other school personnel must develop intervention strategies that are tied to specific behaviors. For example, there are some specific things that teachers can do to help students focus their attention on a learning activity. The Guide to Classroom Intervention included in Appendix A provides an example of linking specific interventions to specific behaviors. The following provides some examples of specific accommodations related to behaviors.

Child's Behavior	Teacher's Accommodations
Difficulty sustaining effort and accuracy over time	• Reduce length of assignment • Strive for quality over quantity • Increase frequency of reinforcement
Difficulty sustaining attention to tasks or other activities	• Reward attention • Break up activities into small units • Use physical proximity and touch • Use study carrels or earphones • Use preferential seating
Poor adult interactions; defies authority	• Provide positive attention • Talk with student individually about inappropriate and appropriate behaviors • Set up contracts

These are just a few examples of intervention techniques that can be used for specific behaviors. A more complete list is in Appendix A. The key thing to remember when determining interventions for students with ADHD is to use a comprehensive approach—do not rely on one method. The best strategy is one that includes making specific accommodations for individual students, using appropriate behavior-management techniques, and taking into consideration group- and physical-management strategies.

Final Thoughts

This chapter has provided an overview of different techniques to use with students with ADHD in classroom situations. Topics presented included group-management techniques, such as controlling the classroom schedule and how to group students; behavior-management techniques, including positive reinforcement, how to decrease inappropriate behaviors, and how to increase appropriate behaviors; and a section on using modifications for specific characteristics.

Students with ADHD present unique challenges to teachers and other school personnel. The techniques presented in this chapter will give teachers some ideas that can be very effective with children who display this condition. While there is no one technique that will be effective with all children, the techniques presented will provide teachers with a repertoire of intervention strategies that can be used to enhance learning for all students.

CHAPTER 5

Accommodating Instructional Needs

Regardless of the exact placement of students with ADHD, a need often arises to make changes in any number of instructionally related areas. The purpose of this chapter is to highlight accommodative practices that can assist students with ADHD in dealing more successfully with the ongoing activities within the classroom and to provide practical examples of useful techniques.

Different terminology is used to describe activities associated with addressing the instructional needs of students with special needs. Terms such as *accommodation, adaptation, modification,* and *alteration* typically are used interchangeably by teachers. To date, a clear distinction among these concepts has not been made. Lambie (1980) provides an informal distinction by associating adaptation with material, modification with instruction, and alteration with assignments. Even though Lambie associates these terms with specific instructional areas where changes may need to be made, she does not define them or discuss their differences. The term *accommodation* is used commonly in the field of special education and human services as an umbrella term for addressing individual needs. For this reason, it is the term of choice for this chapter.

Instructionally related accommodations are organized into four categories in this chapter. This system is an adaptation of a model for curriculum development developed by Maker and Nielson (1996). Figure 5.1 shows the four key domains in which accommodations can be made. The content domain refers to changes in curricular areas relating to the knowledge and skills students learn. Materials accommodations relate to selection, use, and development of specific print and nonprint materials used in classrooms. The instruction domain includes a variety of teacher-directed, student-directed, and peer-directed variables related to the effective delivery of instruction. The last domain involves accommodations associated with assignments given to students and the products they are asked to generate as a part of the learning experience.

Before moving into specific suggestions, it is valuable to provide some general principles for implementing accommodations. These principles cut across the four major domains illustrated in Figure 5.1 and should pervade the day-to-day modus operandi of teachers working in any educational setting where students with ADHD are receiving instruction.

Know yourself and your students. It is imperative that teachers understand their particular perspectives regarding teaching and learning. Moreover, teachers must get to know their students well enough to determine how best to teach them. Serna and Patton (1997) illustrate this point: ". . . [T]eachers must 'know themselves' (e.g., their

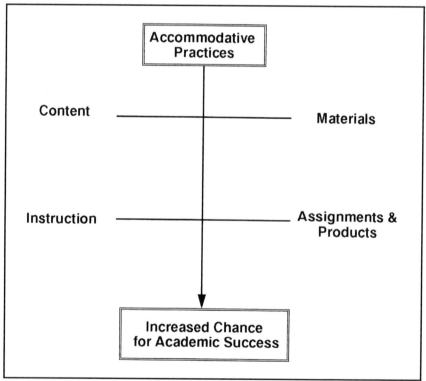

Figure 5.1. Accommodative practices.

beliefs, values, and expectations) and their students (e.g., culture, neighborhood, family, disability) in order to best instruct and meet the needs of these children" (p. 138). The reality of today's classrooms requires teachers to become informed about issues of diversity and their effects on student learning and socialization.

Make accommodations only when needed. There is no need to make changes if they are not needed. Moreover, teachers should start with making minor changes—making major changes only when student needs dictate that more accommodations are required. Teachers simply do not have enough time to make unnecessary accommodations. One way for quickly determining whether accommodations are necessary is the use of classroom-level assessment instruments. The Curriculum Adaptation Quick Screen (CAQS) is an example of such a device. This screen provides a means to quickly identify various instructional dimensions that may require some form of accommodation. The CAQS is shown in Figure 5.2.

Remember that many students can benefit from accommodative practices. Changes to curricular content, instructional materials, instruction, and assignment/products utilized with students with ADHD can benefit other students in the classroom. All of the accommodative practices described in this chapter can assist additional students who may also be experiencing learning-related problems similar to those of students with ADHD.

Ensure that the factors associated with successful inclusive classrooms are being addressed when students are in those settings. Certain characteristics contribute to successful experiences of students who are in inclusive settings, which is the most likely setting for students with ADHD. The following critical dimensions have been found in schools where effective inclusion has occurred (Scruggs and Mastropieri, 1994):

- administrative support is apparent;
- special education support exists;
- open, accepting classroom atmosphere is evident;
- appropriate curriculum is operative;
- effective general teaching skills are displayed;
- peer assistance is available; and
- disability-specific teaching skills are used when necessary.

Curriculum Adaptation Quick Screen (CAQS)

Educator: _____ Student: _____ Subject: _____

Strategy: _____

Class setting: _____

Place a check next to each item for which the student possesses sufficient abilities to work within the classroom relative to the identified subject, strategy, and setting.

Content Needs

☐ Sufficient reading level
☐ Necessary prerequisite skills
☐ Necessary prior experiences
☐ Sufficient language abilities
☐ Sufficient abstract-thinking abilities
☐ Interest in subject area material
☐ Other:

Instructional Strategy Needs

☐ Motivated by strategy used
☐ Strategy generates active student participation
☐ Acquires information through strategy
☐ Understands strategy used
☐ Strategy holds student's attention to task
☐ Other:

Instruction Setting Needs

☐ Able to attend to task within type of setting used
☐ Able to work independently when necessary
☐ Possesses appropriate peer interaction skills for type of setting used
☐ Acquires information easily through setting used
☐ Participates freely in setting
☐ Completes assignments within setting used
☐ Other:

Figure 5.2. Curriculum Adaptation Quick Screen (CAQS). *Note.* From *Curriculum Adaptations for Students with Learning and Behavior Problems* (2nd ed.), by J. J. Hoover and J. R. Patton, 1997, Austin, TX: PRO-ED. Copyright 1997 by PRO-ED, Inc. Reprinted with permission.

Student Behavior

☐ Maintains self-control
☐ Completes assigned tasks on time
☐ Is responsible for own actions
☐ Uses effective self-management techniques
☐ Uses study and learning strategies effectively
☐ Exhibits appropriate behaviors for type of instructional setting used
☐ Other:

Summary of Curriculum Adaptation Needs

Content

_____

_____

_____

Instructional Strategy

_____

_____

_____

Instructional Setting

_____

_____

_____

Student Behaviors

_____

_____

_____

_____

_____

Figure 5.2. Continued.

As can be seen from this list of inclusion criteria, the competence of the teacher is very important; however, some of the critical dimensions are administrative in nature (e.g., support is provided).

Look for new ideas and ways to accommodate individual needs. Innovative ways of dealing with the needs of students with ADHD have been developed, and new practices are emerging regularly, especially in the technology area. Teachers should take advantage of the work of other teachers and already developed resources in addressing the needs of students with ADHD. Professional periodicals, conferences, workshops, projects, and resource materials can provide useful information on accommodative practices (see the appendices to this book).

Evaluate regularly the accommodative capacity of the classroom and the effectiveness of accommodative practices being used. The reevaluation of the types and quality of classroom accommodations as a function of student needs is strongly recommended. It is essential that specific accommodative practices be subjected to close scrutiny. Successful practices should be identified, maintained, and shared among teachers. Ineffective practices must be improved or discarded in favor of other tactics that have a greater chance for producing academic success.

One other issue needs to be discussed prior to the presentation of accommodative practices for addressing the needs of students with ADHD in classroom settings. The issue involves treatment acceptability—the willingness of teachers to implement a specific accommodation. Of greatest concern to teachers is the amount of time any intervention will require, given that there is very little unencumbered time available. In the sections that follow, a number of suggestions are provided for accommodating individual needs. It is important to recognize that, even though teachers support the need to provide accommodations, they often show varying degrees of support for certain recommendations. Sound accommodative practices are useless if teachers do not embrace them. As a result, a realistic appraisal is given of the likelihood that certain recommended practices will be found acceptable to teachers.

The remainder of the chapter discusses specific practices associated with each of the domains depicted in Figure 5.1. A summary listing of the suggested accommodative practices covered in this chapter is provided in Table 5.1.

Table 5.1
List of Accommodative Practices

Content	Materials	Instruction	Assignments/Products
• study skills	• textual material	• learning considerations	• alternative products
• learning strategies	— adapting text	— instructional orientations	• assignment adaptations
• social skills	— enhancing comprehension of existing text	— types of learning	• homework
• related life skills	— retaining information	— appropriate stage of learning	• testing options/modifications
	• adapting other material	• delivery of effective instruction	• grading considerations
	— math material	— teacher location	
	— learning aids	— demonstration, guided practice, independent practice, evaluation paradigm	
	• selecting commercially available materials	— tactics for presenting new information	
		— multisensory activities	
		— lecture-related accommodations	
		— assistive technology	
		• instructional planning	
		— lesson planning	
		— input-output options	
		— grouping	

Curricular Content Accommodations

Curriculum can be defined as the planned and guided learning experiences under the direction of the school. It relates significantly to the content that is covered and that leads to knowledge acquisition and skills development.

Three different types of curricula are possible and are briefly described below (Hoover and Patton, 1997):

explicit curriculum: formal and stated curriculum that teachers and students are expected to follow, as mandated by school boards and state education agencies, and that is documented in curriculum guides;

hidden curriculum: actual curriculum implemented in the classroom—what students actually are exposed to based on teachers' inferences about the explicit curriculum they are required to teach; and

absent curriculum: the curriculum that is not covered in school—i.e., subject areas, specific content, and experiences that are excluded for various reasons.

Understanding that these three types of curricula do exist forces professionals to ponder the issue of what is taught and what is not taught to students while providing a framework to appreciate the many issues that surround curricular accommodations. It is important to realize that what is not taught may be just as important as what is selected to be taught (Eisner, 1985). Because curriculum must be functional by preparing students for the environments in which they will live, work, and learn, certain content areas cannot be excluded.

In addition to the necessity of teaching them certain content, students can be motivated by curricula that they find relevant and meaningful with regard to their daily lives. Kohn (1993) notes that a key condition for developing authentic motivation is the content of the tasks—learning that is contextualized where there is a connection to students' lives and interests. Interestingly, many of the content areas discussed in this section relate well to this notion.

For the most part, the skills discussed in this section are part of the hidden curriculum if they are taught at all. Commonly, these skills are never taught directly to students, with the thinking that students learn these skills incidently. One way to ensure that these important skills are addressed is to include goals related to these areas in the student's IEP or 504 accommodation plan. Another suggestion is to take advantage of courses and special sessions covering these skill areas that some schools provide for students. The ideal situation is the implementation of ongoing coverage of important skill areas. Such programs introduce simple variations of the skills in the primary grades and gradually increase to more complex variations as students progress through school. In other words, critical skills instruction becomes part of the hidden curriculum.

The following discussion highlights a number of content areas that may be excluded from the curriculum to which students with ADHD are exposed. Each of the areas is described and examples of related skills are provided. For most of the areas, select resources are given.

Study Skills

Without question, one of the most important areas in which students with ADHD need to achieve competence is study skills. Study skills are tools for learning and can be described as those specific skills that individuals employ to acquire, record, remember, and use information efficiently. These skills are useful not only in school but in everyday living as well.

A considerable amount of agreement exists as to which specific skills should be considered study skills; however, some disparity can be found across study skills resources. One list of the important study skills and their significance for learning is provided in Table 5.2.

Some useful resources for teaching study skills include: *Teaching Test-Taking Skills: Helping Students Show What They Know* (Scruggs & Mastropieri, 1992); *Teaching Study Strategies to Students with Learning Disabilities* (Strichart & Mangrum, 1993); *Teaching Students with Learning Problems to Use Study Skills: A Teacher's Guide* (Hoover & Patton, 1995).

Learning Strategies

Learning strategies are another set of skills that can be extremely valuable to students. Learning strategies are "task-specific techniques that students use in responding to classroom tasks" (Archer & Gleason, 1995, p. 236). Utilizing a cognitive orientation to learning, these types of strategies provide students with a method for using their own abilities and knowledge to acquire, organize, and integrate new information. Ultimately, successful demonstration of learning strategy competence leads to more self-regulated, independent learning, as these

Table 5.2
Study Skills: Tools for Learning

Study Skill	Significance for Learning
Reading rate	Reading rates vary with type and length of reading assignments.
Listening	Listening skills are necessary to complete most educational tasks or requirements.
Note taking/outlining	Effective note taking and outlining skills allow students to document key points of topics for future study.
Report writing	Report writing is a widely used method for documenting information and expressing ideas.
Oral presentations	Oral presentations provide students an alternative method to express themselves and report information.
Graphic aids	Graphic aids may visually depict complex or cumbersome material in a meaningful format.
Test taking	Effective test-taking abilities help ensure more accurate assessment of student abilities.
Library usage	Library usage skills facilitate easy access to much information.
Reference materials	Independent learning may be greatly improved through effective use of reference materials and dictionaries.
Time management	Time management assists in reducing the number of unfinished assignments and facilitates more effective use of time.
Self-management	Self-management assists students in assuming responsibility for their own behaviors.

Note. From *Teaching Students with Learning Problems to Use Study Skills: A Teacher's Guide* (p. 6), by J. J. Hoover, and J. R. Patton, 1995, Austin, TX: PRO-ED. Copyright 1995 by PRO-ED, Inc. Reprinted with permission.

strategies are generalizable to other situations where a specific task is required. Learning strategy instruction can be particularly helpful to students with ADHD who can benefit from tactics that help them focus on the task at hand.

Many different learning strategies exist, and, accordingly, various systems for organizing learning strategies can be found as well (Archer & Gleason, 1989; Deshler & Lenz, 1989; Hoover & Patton,

1997). Table 5.3 shows general types of learning strategies according to the function the strategy serves, as presented in certain resource materials. A number of formalized strategies are available to assist students with ADHD in dealing with various learning-related tasks, and a select sampling of them is provided in Table 5.4 (see p. 110).

Many of the learning strategies described above are accompanied by a "remembering device" (Archer & Gleason, 1995), which can consist of a word or acronym that relates to the steps one must follow to implement the strategy. Other mnemonic techniques are available for organizing and retrieving information, and these can be taught to students with ADHD. One technique is the use of reconstructive elaborations (Scruggs & Mastropieri, 1994). This technique uses acoustically similar keywords and a graphic representation to link two concepts. For example, in assisting the student to remember the capital of the state of New York, the teacher could associate New York with "new pork" and Albany with "all baloney" and then use the exchange in which a person asks a butcher, "Is this new pork?" and the butcher replies, "It's all baloney." This exchange is coupled with the illustration depicted in Figure 5.3. Therefore, to retrieve the capital of New

Figure 5.3. Mnemonic illustration for teaching the capital of New York. *Note.* From "Applications of Mnemonic Strategies with Students with Mild Mental Disabilities," by M. A. Mastropieri, T. E. Scruggs, M. E. S. Whittaker, and J. P. Bakken, 1994, *Remedial and Special Education,* p. 37. Copyright 1994 by PRO-ED, Inc. Reprinted with permission.

Table 5.3

Types of Learning Strategies as a Function of Primary Operation

Acquiring Information	Organizing Information	Demonstrating Competence
Deshler et al. (1996)		
• word-identification strategy	• first-letter mnemonic strategy	• sentence-writing strategy
• paraphrasing strategy	• paired-associates strategy	• paragraph-writing strategy
• self-questioning strategy	• listening and note-taking strategy	• error-monitoring strategy
• visual-imagery strategy		• theme-writing strategy
• interpreting-visuals strategy		• assignment-completion strategy
• multipass strategy		• test-taking strategy
Archer and Gleason (1989)		
• reading expository material	• gaining information from verbal presentations (lectures, demonstrations)	• completing daily assignments
• reading narrative material		• answering written questions
Hoover and Patton (1997)		• writing narrative and expository products
• active processing		
• analogy	• organization	• preparing for and taking tests
• coping		• rehearsal
• evaluation		

Note. Developed from *Teaching Students with Learning Problems to Use Study Skills: A Teacher's Guide,* by J. J. Hoover and J. R. Patton, 1997, Austin, TX: PRO-ED; *Skills for School Success,* by A. Archer and M. Gleason, 1989, North Billerica, MA: Curriculum Associates; and *Teaching Adolescents with Learning Disabilities: Strategies and Methods,* by D. D. Deshler, E. S. Ellis, and B. K. Lenz, 1996, Denver: Love Publishing.

York, the student thinks of the keyword phrase and relates this to the graphic scene and the other keyword phrase.

The following resources include more extensive coverage of the use and teaching of learning strategies: *Skills for School Success* (Archer & Gleason, 1989); *Teaching Adolescents with Learning Disabilities: Strategies and Methods* (Deshler, Ellis, & Lenz, 1996; Lenz, Ellis, & Scanlon, 1996); *Teaching Students Ways To Remember: Strategies for Learning Mnemonically* (Mastropieri & Scruggs, 1991).

Social Skills

Appropriate social skills are essential for success in school, on the job, and in the community. Social skills refer to the ability to demonstrate behaviors that are socially desirable and to refrain from displaying behaviors that elicit negative responses within the context of two or more persons interacting. Social skills should be proactive, prosocial, and reciprocal in nature so that participants of the interaction share in a mutually rewarding experience. When social skills problems are present, they are of one of four types: total skill deficit—all components of skill are absent; partial skill deficit—some critical elements of the skill are absent; performance deficits—person can demonstrate skill but does not use it at all or with sufficient frequency; and control deficits—undesirable social behaviors (i.e., obtrusive or excessive) are present (Sargent, 1991). Each of these situations requires a more formal approach to social skills development.

All too often, social skills development is not addressed directly within the school curriculum. For many students with special needs, social skills training should be part of the explicit curriculum. In reality, such training is part of the hidden curriculum in many schools because of the ultimate importance of competence in this area.

Important social skills are reflected by the major content areas of existing social skills programs. Skill content covered by some of the more popular curricula is highlighted in Table 5.5.

In addition to the curricula referred to in Table 5.5, some additional resources for teaching social skills include: *Assessment and Instruction of Social Skills* (Elksnin & Elksnin, 1995); *Skillstreaming the Adolescent: A Structured Learning Approach to Teaching Prosocial Skills* (Goldstein, Sprafkin, Gershaw, & Klein, 1980).

Table 5.4
Selected Learning Strategies

Strategy	Task Area	Process	Description
DEFENDS	Written expression	Decide on a specific position Examine own reasons for this position Form list of points explaining each reason Expose position in first sentence of written task Note each reason and associated points Drive home position in last sentence Search for and correct any errors	This strategy helps learners defend a particular position in a written assignment.
PARS	Reading	Preview Ask questions Read Summarize	PARS is recommended for use with younger students and with those who have limited experiences with study strategies.
RAP	Reading comprehension	Read paragraph Ask self to identify the main idea and two supporting details Put main idea and details into own words	This strategy helps students to learn information through paraphrasing.

RDPE	Underlining	Read entire passage Decide which ideas are important Plan the underlining to include only main points Evaluate results of the underlining by reading only the underlined words	This strategy helps learners organize and remember main points and ideas in a reading selection through appropriate underlining of key words.
SCORER	Test taking	Schedule time effectively Clue words identified Omit difficult items until end Read carefully Estimate answers requiring calculations Review work and responses	This test-taking strategy provides a structure for completing various tests by helping students carefully and systematically complete test items.
SQ3R	Reading	Survey Question Read Recite Review	SQ3R provides a systematic approach to improve reading comprehension.
TOWER	Written reports	Think Order ideas Write Edit Rewrite	TOWER provides a structure for completing initial and final drafts of written reports.

Note. Adapted from *Teaching Students with Learning Problems to Use Study Skills: A Teacher's Guide* (pp. 105–107), by J. J. Hoover and J. R. Patton, 1995, Austin, TX: PRO-ED. Copyright 1995 by PRO-ED, Inc. Reprinted with permission.

Table 5.5
Social Skills Content

Social Skills Curricula	School Level	Skill Content Covered
• ACCEPTS Program (Walker et al., 1983)	elementary	classroom skills basic instructions getting along making friends coping skills
• Skillstreaming the Elementary School Child (McGinnis et al., 1984)	elementary	classroom survival friendship making dealing with feelings alternatives to aggression dealing with stress
• ASSET: A Social Skills Program for Adolescents (Hazel et al., 1981)	secondary	giving positive feedback giving negative feedback accepting negative feedback negotiation following instruction problem solving resisting peer pressure conversation
• Social Skills for School and Community (Sargent, 1991)	elementary & secondary	classroom-related skills personal skills interaction-initiative skills interaction-response skills community-related skills work-related skills

Related Life Skills

Another curricular area that might be absent from the educational programs of students with ADHD is that of life skills instruction. The
inclusion of life skills topics can be extremely useful to students currently and in the future. Life skills can be thought of as specific competencies (i.e., knowledge and skills) of local and cultural relevance
needed to perform those events and activities typically encountered
by most adults in everyday life. Without question, life skills competence is needed to deal successfully with the many challenges and
demands of adulthood.

The conceptualization of life skills provided above is broad and includes skills previously discussed in areas such as study skills and social skills. A listing of other life skills would be exhaustive; however, general life skills categories include: daily living, leisure and recreation, community participation and citizenship, transportation, health, self-determination, and occupational preparation.

Life skills instruction may be part of the explicit curriculum in some school districts for some students (i.e., students with mental retardation) but is not typically part of the curriculum for most students. The acquisition of most life skills knowledge and skill competence is left to families and to students themselves. Leaving the acquisition of these skills to chance rather than to a systematic program of study does not contribute to the comprehensive preparation that most students need. While coverage of these important skills is clearly appropriate for noncollege-bound students, these topics are appropriate for college-bound students as well.

Resources that provide descriptions of what life skills should be taught and how to teach them can be found in: *Life-Centered Career Education: A Competency Based Approach* (Brolin, 1991); *Life Skills Activities for Special Children* (Mannix, 1992); *Life Skills Activities for Secondary Students with Special Needs* (Mannix, 1995); and *Life Skills Instruction for All Students with Special Needs: A Practical Guide for Integrating Real-Life Content into the Curriculum* (Cronin & Patton, 1993).

Instructional Materials Accommodations

Many different types of materials are used in school settings. These include a wide variety of print materials that students must be able to read and extract information from for use at a later time. Other nonprint materials such as maps, globes, models, photographs, videos, and computer-based images are also available in school settings. All of these materials can pose problems for students with ADHD.

The key concerns that precipitate the need to make accommodations to instructional materials, for the most part, cut across the different types of materials. These concerns are provided below:

- Student does not display prerequisite skills necessary to handle the material.

- The conceptual complexity of the material exceeds the level at which a student understands. Often the student does not have sufficient background and experience to make sense of the information being presented.

- The linguistic complexity of the material is such that the student is unable to extract meaning from it. Primary sources of problem come from vocabulary and syntactic factors.

- The amount of information presented to students is overwhelming. Typically an emphasis has been placed on breadth of coverage rather than depth of coverage. In reference to textual materials, Deshler, Ellis, and Lenz (1996) note that "even when textbooks are written in ways that 'invite' learning, the sheer volume of information included in textbooks can be overwhelming for teachers and students alike" (p. 417). Students can be overwhelmed by nonprint sources of information as well.

- Far too often the design and format features of materials (e.g., advanced organizers, layout, organization, graphics, cueing, clarity, use of examples, practice opportunities) are lacking or insufficient, thus making the materials difficult to use, especially for students who are encountering learning-related problems. In other words, the "considerateness" (Armbruster & Anderson, 1988) or user-friendliness of materials is frequently in question.

Textual Materials

Text-based materials, for the purpose of this chapter, refer to any type of material that requires reading as the primary means of obtaining information. Text-based materials typically used in classrooms include basal textbooks, workbooks, worksheets, literature, weekly periodicals, handouts, and other reproduced materials. The general cautions previously mentioned hold for these types of materials.

Three general approaches can be implemented to address problems that arise with text-based materials: substitution of some type of alternative material in place of the existing textual material; comprehension enhancement of the existing material; and use of techniques that assist the student in retaining information over time. The first technique aims to avoid the problems associated with existing textual material. The next two approaches are based on ways to assist students while using existing material. The discussion of the various techniques for dealing with textual material, adapted from the recommendations of Schumm and Strickler (1991), offers a number of ideas for addressing problems students may have using textual material along with some concerns associated with the techniques.

Adapting textual material. The primary characteristic of this technique is using an alternative method for conveying the information contained in the textual material being used with students. This approach ranges from the complete substitution of existing text to the modification of the existing text. Some of the suggestions are more likely to be implemented than others due to time, effort, and availability factors.

- Audiotape textual material: Ideally, the material being used is already available through Recordings for the Blind and Dyslexic, and the student can qualify for this service. Otherwise, unless volunteers or other students are available to do the taping, taping may be difficult to do. Lovitt and Horton (1991) do not recommend taping on the basis that "many texts are 'inconsiderate.' . . . It seems apparent that if a passage is disorganized and incoherent, it will continue to be disorganized and incoherent when taped" (p. 443).

- Read the material aloud: This suggestion has the same advantages and limitations as the taping recommendation.

- Pair students to master textual material: This technique has short-term and targeted usefulness and requires the availability of such supports whenever the textual material is being used.

- Use other ways to deliver the material (e.g., direct experiences, media): Other vehicles for delivering information are extremely useful for presenting content-laden topics. The drawback to this idea is the availability of appropriate alternatives and the time to do them.

- Work with students individually or in small groups: This works when students can understand the textual material to some extent and time is available on a regular basis for performing this activity.

- Use a multilevel, multimaterial approach: Textbooks that are written at lower readability levels are available in a number of content areas. Other supplementary reading materials that are written at a lower reading level can also be introduced. This approach allows students to remain in a specific course and gain the information they need through the use of materials they can handle. This technique is enhanced by the use of some of the other suggestions previously discussed.

- Develop abridged versions of textual content: The attractiveness of this suggestion is that students are able to use textual material that is suited to their reading levels. The fact that this type of material almost always needs to be developed (i.e., written) by the teacher or other personnel is a drawback due to the time and energy involved. It is for this reason that Lovitt and Horton (1991) do not recommend this technique.

- Simplify existing textual material: To deal with vocabulary, terminology, and expressions that are difficult for students to understand, the teacher can simplify them. In place of rewriting complete textual passages, one can place a transparency over a page of written material and, with a marker, cross out the more difficult words and substitute more understandable equivalents in the margin (Hoover & Patton, 1997).

Enhancing comprehension. A variety of ways exist to assist students in better understanding what they read. This may be especially important for students with ADHD. The following recommendations focus on tactics for improving comprehension of textual material, particularly grade-level material.

- Provide students with purposes for the reading they are being asked to do: This simply helps students appreciate what the goal of the reading assignment is.

- Preview the reading assignment: This very important activity, which too often is omitted, prepares students for some of the specifics of what they will encounter. This prereading activity should introduce the students to new vocabulary and concepts that they will encounter and that may pose problems. The use of a diagram or story frame may be helpful.

- Teach students how to use format features: An extremely useful set of skills includes the ability to use headings, bold-face type, visual aids (e.g., figures, tables, exhibits, photographs), opening sections, and summaries of textual material to gain an organization and additional meaning from the textual material.

- Engage the student prior to reading: Stimulating thinking about what is to be read is extremely helpful. The use of an anticipation guide that asks students certain questions that will be answered during the course of their reading is one such tactic.

- Use a study guide: Some commercial textbooks provide these supplementary aids; other texts do not. The primary objective of using this type of aid is to guide the students through the reading material by having them respond to questions or statements related to the passages they are reading or have read. Study guides are a way of organizing and guiding the comprehension of textual material.

• Utilize graphic organizers: These techniques use visual formats or structures to help students organize information for better comprehension. Specific techniques include the use of a central-story-problem format, story frames or story map, and semantic mapping. An example of a story map is presented in Figure 5.4.

Sample Story Map
Title: *Cinderella (Perrault/Jeffers)*

Characters:

Cinderella

Stepmother, father

2 Stepsisters

Fairy Godmother, prince

Setting:

Time: Long ago

Place: Kingdom

Problem:

Father dies, Cinderella mistreated and
not allowed to go to the king's ball.

Goal:

To go to the ball and meet the handsome
prince.

Events to Reach Solution:

1. Fairy Godmother changes Cinderella's rags into ballgown and glass slippers and sends her to the ball in exchange for her promise to be back by midnight.

2. Cinderella dances with the prince at the ball, forgetting the time.

3. As the clock strikes 12, she runs from the ball, losing a glass slipper.

4. Cinderella is changed back into her rags.

5. The prince searches for the girl whose foot fits the glass slipper.

Solution:

Cinderella can wear the slipper. When she puts on the matching one, she turns back into the way she looked at the ball. She leaves with the prince to be married and live happily ever after.

Figure 5.4. Sample story map. *Note.* Adapted from "Constructing Meaning: An Integrated Approach to Teaching Reading," by K. D. Barclay, 1990, *Intervention in School and Clinic, 26,* p. 88. Copyright 1990 by PRO-ED, Inc. Reprinted with permission.

- Modify the nature of the reading assignment: It might be necessary to reduce the length of the assigned reading or to slow down the pace of content being covered.

- Highlight the textual material: If it is possible to highlight the actual textual material prior to a student using the material, a teacher can focus the reader on important points in the passage. Highlighting can also be used prior to reading by having the student go through the text and highlight all headings, thus introducing the reader to what will be encountered.

- Teach comprehension-monitoring strategies: Various strategies have been developed to help students think about how well they are understanding what they are reading and how they can address any problems they are having.

- Adapt text-based activities: Reorganizing and rewriting the "end of chapter" questions that are often included with textbooks may be needed. For students who are experiencing reading problems, these types of questions can be very frustrating. Chalmers (1992) provides examples of how to make these types of modifications.

Retaining information acquired through text. As Schumm and Strickler (1991) note, "Some students can read the words and can comprehend material during ongoing reading . . . nonetheless, some students do not perform well on tests due to difficulty with long-term memory" (p. 83). Whether the need is test-related, which is an important reality, or for general knowledge, ways to assist students to retain what they have read are needed.

- Utilize graphic aids: Various types of visual organizers can be used in the postreading phase.

- Incorporate formal learning strategies: Some specific strategies that include a retention component can be taught to students. Table 5.4 lists some of these strategies. Most techniques ask the student to write a short description of the main points or a summary of what they read.

- Teach test-preparation skills: An assortment of skills that are needed to prepare for tests work in conjunction with material that has been read. In most secondary and postsecondary settings, it is assumed that students can handle the reading material and use what has been read to respond successfully to questions that are asked on tests.

- Teach class-discussion preparation skills: Much like successful test performance, contributing to class discussions can require preparation, especially for students who struggle with reading the textual material on which the discussions will be based. Structured ways of organizing information may be needed.

Adapting Other Instructional Materials

Other types of curricular materials may pose problems for students with ADHD.

Math materials. The primary concerns addressed in this section on math materials relate to the use of the basal textbook approach that is used in most schools. If the challenges associated with using this approach to teaching math are recognized, solutions can be implemented. The key factors that teachers must consider when using math texts with students who are experiencing problems include:

- instructor's manuals do not provide specific teaching strategies for teaching a given skill;

- sufficient practice may not be provided;

- movement from one skill/topic to another may be too rapid;

- sometimes there is not enough review of previously covered topics;

- linguistic and conceptual demands may inhibit understanding— the issues of text-based material are relevant in math as well;

- variety of the types of activities that students do is limited;

- activities and content are not relevant to students; and

- problem-solving applications are often too contrived. (Polloway & Patton, 1997)

The availability of other math resources such as *Project MATH* (Cawley et al., 1976) and *Direct Instruction Mathematics* (Silbert, Carnine, & Stein, 1990) can be used effectively to address many of the presenting problems noted above.

Learning aids. Brief mention needs to be given to any type of learning aid (e.g., outside readings, realia, games, learning centers, in-class projects) that might be part of an instructional program. Caution must be exercised to ensure that students know how to use these materials. If textual material is part of the learning aid, various suggestions offered above may need to be included. In regard to the use of instructional games, students need to possess appropriate game-playing skills and behaviors—this is extremely critical if students play games in cooperative situations without direct teacher involvement or monitoring.

Selecting Commercially Available Materials

The selection and use of instructional materials is a key element of the teaching process. This process includes a number of stages: determination of need, availability, evaluation, actual ordering, and use. While all of these aspects of material selection are important and suggestions can be offered (see Polloway & Patton, 1997), this section focuses on the evaluation component. To assist teachers in performing this important activity, resources are provided.

Figure 5.5 is a tool for evaluating instructional materials. Given the great time demands teachers have, a succinct method for examining instructional materials is useful. This particular device fulfills this need.

In evaluating software and other computer-based media (e.g., CD-ROM), other systems are needed. One tool for doing this is the *SECTOR Courseware Evaluation Form* (Reid, Allard, & Hofmeister, 1993). The major components of this form are: general product description, content (including items related to target audience), instructional design, record keeping and management, ease of use, program strengths and weaknesses, and validation. This type of comprehensiveness is warranted when examining the exploding amount of computer-based materials.

Instructional Practices Accommodations

This section is about good teaching. No attempt is made to cover all of what is known about best and recommended practice. The purpose of this section is to remind us of certain elements of effective teaching that are needed to optimize the learning environment for students with ADHD.

Material Evaluation Form

Name of curriculum or material _____

Copyright date _____ Publisher _____

Area of instruction _____

Intended audience (age and/or grade) _____

Date of evaluation _____

Evaluator _____

Rate each of the questions with the following scale:

1. Material meets the intent of the statement
2. Material would be appropriate with modifications
3. Material does not meet the intent of the statement and alternative materials should be found

	Ratings	Comments
I. Scope and Sequence		
1. The declarative knowledge included in this material is appropriate for the students.	1 2 3	
2. The procedural knowledge included in this material is appropriate for the students.	1 2 3	
3. The stated objectives taught in the program seem to be sequenced correctly.	1 2 3	
4. The material includes all objectives necessary for the mastery of the content.	1 2 3	
5. The material includes objectives focusing on higher-order skills (application and generalization).	1 2 3	
II. Organization		
1. Data-based evaluation		
A. The material includes pre- and posttests.	1 2 3	
B. Criteria for mastery levels are clearly noted, including acquisition, proficiency, and automaticity.	1 2 3	

(Continues)

Figure 5.5. Form used in evaluating and adapting curricular materials. *Note.* From "Curriculum Evaluation and Modification: An Effective Teaching Perspective," by L. Reisberg, 1990, *Intervention in School and Clinic, 26,* p. 101. Copyright 1990 by PRO-ED, Inc. Reprinted with permission.

	Ratings		Comments
C. Suggestions for branching and acceleration are included.	1 2 3		
2. Appropriate time lines and pacing			
A. Time allotted for each lesson is appropriate.	1 2 3		
B. Pacing for each objective is appropriate for students.	1 2 3		
3. Input and output requirements are appropriate.	1 2 3		
III. Presentation			
1. Lessons begin with a daily review.	1 2 3		
2. The objective for each lesson is clearly presented to the students.	1 2 3		
3. An overview of the lesson and activities is presented.	1 2 3		
4. The presentation follows a clear format.	1 2 3		
5. Student attention and interest are maintained.	1 2 3		
6. Skills are modeled for students.	1 2 3		
7. Instruction progresses from concrete to abstract examples.	1 2 3		
8. Frequent and varied questions are posed.	1 2 3		
9. Clear correction procedures are described.	1 2 3		
10. Presentation is at appropriate instructional level.	1 2 3		
IV. Guided Practice			
1. Provides sufficient practice opportunities.	1 2 3		
2. Sets mastery levels at the proficiency level.	1 2 3		
V. Independent Practice			
1. Includes active seatwork practice.	1 2 3		
2. Sets mastery at the automatic stage.	1 2 3		
3. Focus on generalization.	1 2 3		
VI. Periodic Review			
1. Presents skill in both familiar and novel situations.	1 2 3		

Figure 5.5. Continued.

Learning Considerations

Three different instructional orientations are available: teacher-directed, student-directed, and peer-directed. Most teachers use all three orientations in their classrooms. The important point is that each orientation has a set of expectations and procedures that teachers must recognize and students must understand. All three orientations are valid and should be considered in delivering sound instruction to students with ADHD.

Another learning-related issue that teachers must understand is the different types of learning. The reason this is important is because certain instructional conditions and adaptations are required for each type of learning as they are used with students with special needs. Mastropieri and Scruggs (1994) identify the different types of learning as: discrimination learning, factual learning, rule learning, procedural learning, and conceptual learning. Each type of learning is used in school and home. Academic and social examples of each type of learning are presented in Table 5.6.

In working with students with ADHD, attention should also be given to the stages of learning. Many problems arise when these basic stages of learning are ignored or misapplied. The primary stages or levels of learning are: acquisition, proficiency, maintenance, and generalization. It is crucial to recognize the aim of each stage and to apply it appropriately in instructional contexts. A brief description of each stage and its primary aim are found in Table 5.7.

Delivery of Effective Instruction

When teaching students who have ADHD, teachers should implement the basic elements of effective teaching. Some of the more important points to review are discussed below:

- Capitalize on location: Proximity to students who are experiencing learning-related problems can assist those students to attend to the important dimensions of what is occurring in the classroom, give them easier access to support, and minimize behavioral problems that might arise.

- Utilize the demonstration-guided, practice-independent, practice-evaluation paradigm: Highly effective for maximizing the proba-

Table 5.6

Types of Learning

Learning Type	Reading	Arithmetic	Social
Discrimination	*p* vs. *q*	+ vs. −	cooperate vs. compete
Factual			
Associative	*l* = *ell*	5 + 2 = 7	Laughing at other people is rude.
Serial list	a, b, c, d, e . . .	2, 4, 6, 8, 10, 12 . . .	School song or motto.
Rule	If two vowels appear together, say the long sound of the first vowel.	Two divide fractions, invert and multiply.	Do unto others as you would have other do unto you.
Concept	vowel	prime number	courtesy
Procedure	1. Read title 2. Self-question 3. Skim passage 4. Self-question 5. Read carefully 6. Answer questions	1. Count decimal places in division. 2. Move decimal point in divisor that many places to the right, insert caret. 3. Place decimal point directly above caret in quotient.	1. Walk quietly in line. 2. Take tray, utensils, and napkins. 3. Put lunch on tray. 4. Take carton of milk. 5. Walk quietly to lunch table.

Table 5.7
Stages of Learning

Acquisition

The learner is in the process of acquiring but has not acquired the skill. The learner has no knowledge of how to perform the task accurately and therefore never responds correctly, no matter how many times he or she is tested. In this stage the teacher offers direct instruction, followed by practice in the skill area. Modeling may be used here.

The aim of instruction is *accuracy* of response.

Proficiency

The learner responds accurately but with insufficient speed. The learner performs accurately, indicating acquisition of the requisite information but needs to perform the skill quickly enough to be practically automatic, so that other skills may be built upon this one and not be impeded by slow performance.

The aim of instruction is for the teacher to reinforce the learner for faster *rates* of response.

Maintenance

The learner is expected to retain both accuracy and fluency with the skill. The learner may or may not continue to perform at a proficient level. Consequently, the teacher must periodically evaluate retention and again use direct instruction when necessary to maintain both accuracy and speed of response.

The aim of instruction is *retention* of the skill.

Generalization

The learner is expected to transfer the skill to new situations or settings, regardless of the setting or response mode required. The teacher provides direct instruction in alternate settings and response modes when the student fails to generalize. The teacher programs for generalization in different settings and modes, varying stimulus conditions, telling students which to attend to and which to ignore, as well as training other personnel in alternative settings to maintain similar procedures.

The aim of instruction is *expansion* of the skill across situations, behaviors, and time.

Note. Adapted from "The Resource/Consulting Teacher: An Integrated Model of Service Delivery," by L. Idol, 1989, *Remedial and Special Education, 10*(6), p. 41. Copyright 1989 by PRO-ED, Inc. Adapted with permission.

bility that a skill will be learned, this method includes the following sequence of stages: the teacher demonstrates the behavior or skill to be taught; the student is then given an opportunity to perform the behavior with guidance from the teacher (This phase may include the use of physical, verbal, visual, or gestural prompts.); the student eventually practices the behavior without assistance. Ultimately, an adequate evaluation of performance is undertaken.

- Take great care in presenting new information: Mastropieri and Scruggs (1993) have identified six factors that are crucial for teaching new information to students. They refer to them as the SCREAM variables: structure, clarity, redundancy, enthusiasm, appropriate pace, and maximize engagement.

- Use multisensory experiences: The statements that multisensory activities can have a drastic impact on learning, as some people claim, should not deter from the fact that such activities can be instructionally useful.

- Make needed lecture-related accommodations: Much attention has been given already to text-based issues. Just as important is the need to attend to adaptations that might be needed in lecture-type settings. Teacher-controlled adaptations include scheduling the session so more breaks are possible, organizing the lecture so that a variety of instructional methods (e.g., discussion, media) are utilized, moving around the room, being responsive to the audience and specific students, highlighting important points, and providing advanced organizers. The use of preparatory activities like those used in enhancing comprehension of text are applicable here as well. In addition, note-taking skills and listening strategies may need to be taught. If the lecture format allows for discussion, then the student may also need to develop better question-asking skills.

- Use assistive technology: Familiarity with the range of assistive technology (AT) options is warranted. AT ranges from low-tech applications (e.g., tape player) to high tech (e.g., FM systems for helping students concentrate on what is being said). Without question, the use of AT with students who are ADHD may make a substantial difference in the learning of those students. Teachers should know what devices are available, how to have a student evaluated, and, if such devices are used, how they work.

Instructional Planning

Three elements need to be discussed in relation to planning. First, lesson plans should include a section on accommodating students who have learning-related needs. One suggestion is to include a section on special needs as part of the lesson planning form.

The second issue is the use of different input and output modes in teaching. There are two benefits: It allows the teacher to address the needs of students; and it introduces variety. Cawley, Fitzmaurice-Hays, and Shaw (1988) developed the idea of the interactive unit. This formulation was incorporated into many of the math materials that he developed. A variation of this model is illustrated in Figure 5.6. In this model, *input* refers to the way the student receives information, and *output* refers to the way the student acts on this information. As can be seen, for most topical areas for which planning is needed, 24 options exist for developing instructional activities and experiences.

The third issue related to planning is grouping. In peer-oriented learning situations such as cooperative learning arrangements, students with ADHD will need to display a host of skills to be successful. When planning instruction and deciding on grouping arrangements, teachers need to consider a number of factors: purpose for the grouping, group size, physical conditions, student characteristics, and, as mentioned, the requisite academic and social (e.g., cooperative) skills.

Assignment and Products Accommodations

This final component of the instructional accommodation process involves practices that relate to the assignments that are given, the types of products that are possible, and the ways they are evaluated. Five topics are presented for which some suggestions are given. These five areas are: alternative product ideas, assignment adaptations and management, homework issues, testing options, and the monitoring and evaluation of performance.

Alternative Products

For some time, professionals in the field of gifted education have promoted the idea of a variety of product options. Perhaps it is time that

Student Input/Output Options

Output: Input:	Writes	Talks	Makes	Performs	Solves	Identifies
Reads						
Listens						
Views						
Does						

Figure 5.6. Student input/output options. *Note.* Adapted from *Mathematics for the Mildly Handicapped: A Guide to Curriculum and Instruction,* by J. F. Cawley; A. M. Fitzmaurice-Hayes, and R. A. Shaw, 1988, Boston: Allyn & Bacon, and from *Facilitator Manual, Teacher Training Program: Mainstreaming Mildly Handicapped Students in the Regular Classroom,* by P. B. Smith and G. Bentley, 1975, Austin, TX: Education Service Center, Region XII.

those of us who work with students who are ADHD think along those lines as well. To give students options and some choice about those options is desirable practice. All too often teachers tend to make the same assignments to all students. For students who have ADHD, and who have strengths in areas in which they are seldom allowed to show their ability, having alternative products might allow expression of those strengths.

The notion of having different outcomes for students fits with the previously discussed concept of input and output modes. Some examples of various alternative products that could be used are depicted in Table 5.8.

Assignment Adaptations

Frequently, it will become necessary to alter the assignments so that students with certain learning-related problems can handle what is assigned. Teachers can alter assignments in the following ways: shorten assignments (i.e., break them into smaller versions), change the criterion that designates successful completion of the assignment, allow more time to complete the assignment, reduce the difficulty of the content, and change the output mode.

Each of these adaptations can be beneficial to the student with ADHD. The important point is that none of these adaptations should be made if it is not needed; if one is needed, the least amount of change possible is desirable.

A good example of the need for assignment adaptation is a page from a math workbook of 16 subtraction algorithms involving money values, which has been given to students to complete. For a student who is experiencing difficulty with this type of activity but who is capable of doing the math, some type of adaptation is needed.

Homework

A staple of the education diet is homework. Most of the literature supports the use of homework as having a desirable effect on school learning. While homework may present special problems for students with ADHD and their families, certain homework-related suggestions can result in beneficial outcomes. Table 5.9 highlights 34 suggestions related to giving homework to students who have ADHD.

Table 5.8

Product Ideas

Advertisement	Museum
Annotated bibliography	Musical composition
Board game	Oral report or speech
Book	Overhead transparency
Chart or graph	Pamphlet or brochure
Collage	Panel discussion
Collection	Paper folding
Comic strip	Photo essay
Computer program	Photo album
Crossword puzzle	Play or skit
Dance	Poem
Demonstration	Portfolio of artwork
Display	Poster or bumper sticker
Diorama	Puppet show
Dictionary or glossary	Radio show
Diary	Recipe
Experiment	Sample specimens
Film	Scavenger hunt
Illustrated story	Scrapbook
Invention	Sculpture
Guest speaker	Slide show
Jigsaw puzzle	Song (original)
Letter	Tape recording
Magazine or newspaper	Terrarium
Map with key	Timeline
Mini center	Travelogue
Mobile	TV program
Model	Written paper
Mural	Video

Note. From "Product Development for Gifted Students," by K. R. Stephens, 1996, *Gifted Child Today Magazine, 19*(6), p. 19. Copyright 1996 by Prufrock Press. Reprinted with permission.

Testing Options and Modifications

Another area that is of great interest to teachers and parents is testing. While there may be no clean solution to how to test students with special needs appropriately and with fairness to them and to their peers, some adaptive practices can be made. Polloway, Bursuck, Jayanthi, Epstein, and Nelson (1996) have conducted a series of

Table 5.9
Recommended Homework Practices

Management considerations

Assess student homework skills

Involve parents from the outset

Assign homework from the beginning of the year

Schedule time and establish a routine for assigning, collecting, and evaluating homework

Communicate the consequences for not completing assignments

Minimize the demands of teacher time

Coordinate with other teachers

Present homework instructions clearly

Verify the assignment given

Allow students to start homework in class

Use assignment books and/or folders

Implement classroom-based incentive programs

Have parents sign and date homework

Evaluate assignments

Assignment considerations

Recognize the purpose of the homework assignment

Establish relevance

Use appropriate stage-of-learning demands

Select appropriate type of activity

Keep assignments from getting too complex or novel

Ensure reasonable chance of completion and high rate of success

Adapt assignment as needed

Avoid using homework as punishment

Consider nonacademic assignments

Student competencies

Demonstrate minimum levels of competence

Possess academic support skills

Promote interdependent learning

Develop self-management skills

Foster responsibility

Parent involvement

Serve in a supportive role

Go through training, if available

Create a home environment that is conducive to doing homework

Encourage and reinforce student effort

Maintain ongoing involvement

Communicate views regarding homework to school personnel

Note. From "Practical Recommendations for Using Homework for Students with Learning Disabilities," by J. R. Patton, 1994, *Journal of Learning Disabilities, 27,* p. 573. Copyright 1994 by PRO-ED, Inc. Reprinted with permission.

studies related to homework, grading, and testing. In the course of their research, they identified the testing adaptations that teachers thought were the most helpful to students. This ranking, presented in Table 5.10, is a useful resource for making testing adaptations.

Grading Considerations

Along with testing and homework, grading is one of the most frequently discussed topics related to students with special needs. Polloway and colleagues (1996) also identified which adaptations teachers thought were most helpful to students with disabilities; this ranking is shown in Table 5.11.

An example of a way to blend some of the grading suggestions that teachers believe are helpful is to use an ongoing student evaluation report. This type of document, an example of which is shown in Figure 5.7, allows for regular feedback on three dimensions organized across subject areas and can be modified to address the requirements of a given school system.

Final Thoughts

This chapter covers one of the most critical elements of the intervention process for students with ADHD—instructional accommodation. The chapter organized instructional accommodation into four primary areas where changes can be made: curriculum, materials, instructional process, and assignments and products. Although the suggestions presented in this chapter cover a wide range of potential needs and a specific student with ADHD may require only some of these suggestions, the content of this chapter in conjunction with assessment practices discussed in Chapter 3 can serve as a useful resource for teachers. Instructional accommodations along with environmental management and student-directed behaviors are the framework of school-based services for students with ADHD.

Table 5.10

Teachers' Ratings of Helpfulness of Testing Adaptations

Rank[a]	Adaptation
1	Give individual help with directions during tests.
2	Read test questions to students.
3	Simplify wording of test questions.
4	Give practice questions as a study guide.
5	Give extra help preparing for tests.
6	Give extended time to finish tests.
7	Use black-and-white copies.
8	Give feedback to individual student during test.
9	Highlight key words in questions.
10	Allow use of learning aids during tests (e.g., calculators).
11	Give frequent quizzes rather than only exams.
12	Allow students to answer fewer questions.
13	Allow oral instead of written answers (e.g., via tape recorders).
14	Give the actual test as a study guide.
15	Change question type (e.g., essay to multiple choice).
16	Teach students test-taking skills.
17	Use tests with enlarged print.
18	Test individual on less content than rest of class.
19	Provide extra space on tests for answering.
20	Give tests in small groups.
21	Give open-book/notes tests.
22	Allow word processors.
23	Allow answers in outline format.
24	Give take-home tests.

Note. From "Treatment Acceptability: Determining Appropriate Interventions Within Inclusive Classrooms," by E. A. Polloway, W. D. Bursuck, M. Jayanthi, M. H. Epstein, and J. S. Nelson, 1996, *Intervention in School and Clinic, 31,* p. 140. Copyright 1996 by PRO-ED, Inc. Reprinted with permission.

[a]Ranked from most helpful to least helpful by general education teachers.

Table 5.11

Teachers' Ratings of Helpfulness of Specific
Grading Adaptations for Students with Disabilities

Rank[a]	Adaptation
1	Separate grades are given for process (e.g., effort) and product (e.g., tests).
2	Grades are based on the amount of improvement an individual makes.
3	Grades are based on meeting IEP objectives.
4	Grading weights are adjusted (e.g,. efforts on projects count more than tests).
5	Grades are adjusted according to student ability.
6	Grades are based on meeting the requirements of academic or behavioral contracts.
7	Grades are based on less content than the rest of the class.
8	Grades are based on a modified grading scale (e.g., from 93 to 100 = A, 90 to 100 = A).
9	Students are passed if they make an effort to pass.
10	Students are passed no matter what.

Note. From "Treatment Acceptability: Determining Appropriate Interventions Within Inclusive Classrooms," by E. A. Polloway, W. D. Bursuck, M. Jayanthi, M. H. Epstein, and J. S. Nelson, 1996, *Intervention in School and Clinic, 31,* p. 138. Copyright 1996 by PRO-ED, Inc. Reprinted with permission.

[a]Ranked from most helpful to least helpful by general education teachers.

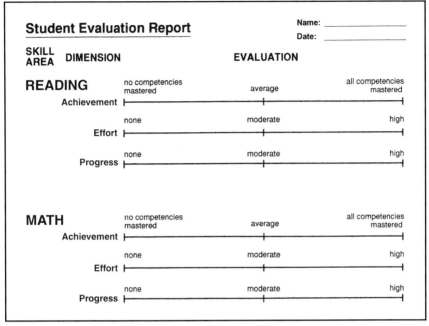

Figure 5.7. Student evaluation report.

CHAPTER 6

Developing Student-Regulated Strategies

An important general area of intervention to be considered for students with attention-deficit disorder and hyperactivity is based on student regulation. *Student-regulated strategies* can be defined as interventions that, though initially taught by the teacher, are intended to be implemented independently by the student. The concept is an outgrowth of the emerging focus on cognitive behavior modification, which has been a popular and exciting option for educational intervention for students with disabilities since the early 1980s.

A number of the behavioral characteristics associated with ADHD are particularly important for their potential relationship to self-regulated, cognitive interventions. These include those associated with attentional problems as well as with the general construct of impulsivity. Zentall (1993) clearly identifies a variety of specific problems within the attention-deficit and impulsivity domain that warrant close attention in designing interventions. These characteristics include:

- academic errors stemming from an individual's failure to consider alternative information in problem solving
- failure to wait, leading to poor test performance; poor skill in planning; limited organizational skills; and failure to read directions
- reduced likelihood of seeking assistance and/or difficulty in the formulation of requests for assistance (e.g., from teachers)

Collectively, these characteristics underscore the importance of teaching individuals with attentional disorders strategies that promote a reflective, cognitively active learning style.

Fiore, Becker, and Nero (1993) state the clear rationale for self-regulatory interventions in their discussion of cognitive approaches. As these authors note, "Although behavior therapy offers a limited but time-tested and practical course for educators, cognitive-behavioral therapy is the most intuitively appealing intervention because it combines behavioral techniques with cognitive strategies designed to directly address core problems of impulse control, higher order problem solving, and self-regulation" (p. 166). The intuitive appeal of cognitive interventions is apparent. Specifically, while traditional behavioral interventions most often stress the importance of teacher monitoring of student behavior, extrinsic reinforcement, and teacher-directed learning, cognitive interventions include a student-regulation focus and stress teaching students to monitor their own behavior, to engage in self-reinforcement, and to direct their own learning in strategic fashion. As Reeve (1990) stresses, the historical emphasis on stimulus reduction and behavior management interventions in this field often inadvertently led to dependence by students on others to manage their learning environment.

A variety of educational interventions have been encouraged in the domain of student regulation for students with attention deficits and related learning problems. The rationales for the use of such strategies with students with attentional problems are clear. They offer the promise of enhancing the educational development of students with ADHD by:

- increasing their selective attention/focus

- modifying their impulsive responding

- providing them with verbal mediators to assist in academic and social problem-solving situations

- teaching them effective self-instructional statements to enable them to "talk through" tasks and problems

- providing strategies that may lead to improvement in peer relations and the development of prosocial behaviors (Rooney, 1993)

In spite of the intuitive appeal of cognitive interventions, Fiore et al. (1993) signal the cautions that have arisen in relationship to such interventions. The concern that they express is based on the fact that research support for cognitive interventions for individuals who are identified as ADHD has by no means been consistently positive. For example, Abikoff (1991) has raised serious questions about the demonstrated effectiveness of such approaches. While the benefits of cognitive interventions have not been sufficiently well demonstrated to argue for the wholesale adoption of cognitive approaches, nevertheless practice still argues for their consideration, tempered by the need for further study (Fiore et al., 1993).

The authors of this book find the potential classroom applications of cognitive interventions to be powerful. The effectiveness of such approaches for students with varied behavioral disorders (see Nelson, Smith, Young, and Dodd, 1991) further argues for their consideration. However, given the relative newness of the ADHD field, practitioners are encouraged to evaluate and document the effectiveness of specific cognitive interventions as they use them in the classroom (Abikoff, 1991; Nelson et al., 1991; Pfiffner & Barkley, 1990; Reeve, 1990). We offer the following list of cautions for practitioners:

- While the key focus is on internalized self-regulation, the actual achievement of internalization remains speculative.

- Generalization and maintenance effects have not as yet been clearly demonstrated in students with ADHD.

- Instructional procedures must include opportunities for students to apply skills in different situations, since such generalization may not occur spontaneously.

- Advocacy for cognitive interventions requires a corresponding specific commitment to train for generalization (thus avoiding a "train and hope" philosophy). There is clear value in training directly in home or classroom vs. training solely in a clinical setting due to the problem of transfer of training. The established effectiveness of specific interventions with certain populations (e.g., learning disabled students) must nevertheless be tempered with caution regarding the generalization of effects across populations (e.g., to ADHD students).

- The multiple problems of children with ADHD most often require combinations of treatments.

Four topics concerning student-regulated strategies will be discussed in the following pages: self-management, learning strategies, study and organizational tactics, and social skills.

Self-Management

The central goal of self-management or self-control programs is to "try and make children more consciously aware of their other thinking processes and task approach strategies, and to give them responsibility for their own reinforcement" (Reeve, 1990, p. 76). Lloyd, Landrum, and Hallahan (1991, p. 201) cited the advantages of teaching self-control as including:

- increasing the effectiveness of an intervention
- decreasing the demand for direct intervention by teachers, saving their time
- improving the maintenance of treatment effects
- increasing the chances of transfer of treatment effects

Implicit in self-management are a variety of mechanisms that can be considered within the context of self-regulation. These include the following:

- *Self-assessment:* the individual determines the need for change and subsequently monitors or charts his or her personal behavior.
- *Self-monitoring:* the student specifically attends to his or her own behavior, such as attention paying or academic performance.
- *Self-instruction:* the student uses self-cuing to inhibit certain inappropriate behaviors and to direct appropriate ones.
- *Self-reinforcement:* the student takes primary responsibility for selecting reinforcers so that they can be self-administered, contingent on performance of the specified appropriate behavior (Gardner, 1977; Polloway & Patton, 1997).

A helpful model for conceptualizing self-management is presented by Workman and Katz (1995). Figure 6.1 illustrates this model.

Two strategies that are worthy of further attention are self-monitoring and self-instruction. *Self-monitoring* has been an intervention commonly employed with students with learning problems. Lloyd and colleagues (1991) note that self-monitoring was initially seen as an assessment technique but that as clients observed their own

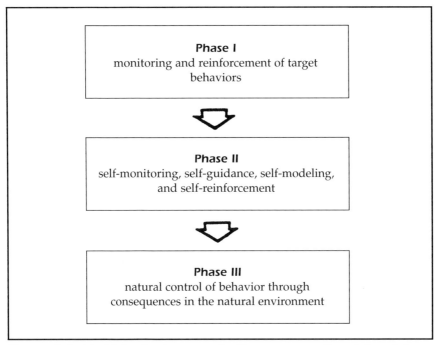

Figure 6.1. Model for development of self-management. *Note.* Adapted from *Teaching Behavioral Self-Control to Students* (2nd ed., p.7), by A. E. Workman and A. M. Katz, 1995, Austin, TX: PRO-ED, Inc.

behavior, the process of observation also resulted in a change in their behavior. As Lloyd et al. and Polloway and Patton (1993) note in their reviews of the literature in this area, self-monitoring, such as of attention, is a relatively simple technique that has been validated with children who have learning disabilities, mental retardation, multiple disabilities, and behavior disorders as well as with those who are not disabled. The subsequent effect of increased attention, achieved through self-monitoring, on academic achievement has also been reported.

A common mechanism for self-monitoring was developed by Hallahan, Lloyd, and Stoller (1982) and involves a series of classroom-based techniques. It consists of the use of a tape-recorded tone that sounds at random intervals, averaging every forty-five seconds, and a self-recording sheet. Children are instructed to ask themselves, each time the tone sounds, whether they are paying attention and then to mark the yes or no box on the self-recording sheet (see Figure 6.2).

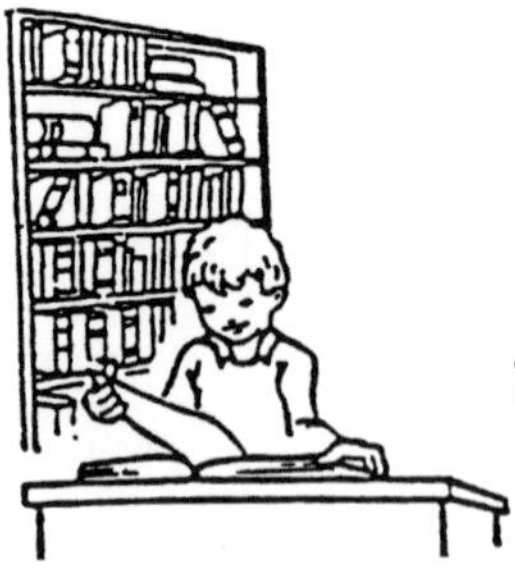

DATE ____________

Was I paying attention?

1	11
2	12
3	13
4	14
5	15
6	16
7	17
8	18
9	19
10	20

Figure 6.2. Self-monitoring recording sheet. *Note.* From *Improving Attention with Self-Monitoring: A Manual for Teachers* (p. 27), by D. P. Hallahan, J. W. Lloyd, and L. Stoller, 1982, Charlottesville, VA: University of Virginia. Copyright 1982 by University of Virginia Learning Disabilities Research Institute. Reprinted with permission.

Other mechanisms are also available. For example, Prater, Joy, Chilman, Temple, and Miller (1991) recommended a pictorial cue, while Dunlap, Dunlap, Koegel, and Koegel (1991) developed an alternative self-monitoring device (see Figures 6.3 and 6.4).

Katy's Self-Monitoring Checklist										
Step	Problem Number									
	1	2	3	4	5	6	7	8	9	10
1. I copied the problem correctly.										
2. I regrouped when I needed to.										
3. I borrowed correctly. (The number crossed out is 1 bigger.)										
4. I subtracted all of the numbers.										
5. I subtracted correctly.										

Figure 6.3. Self-monitoring visual prompt. *Note.* From "Self-Monitoring of On-Task Behavior by Adolescents with Learning Disabilities," by M. A. Prater, R. Joy, B. Chilman, J. Temple, and S. R. Miller, 1991, *Learning Disability Quarterly, 14,* p. 169. Copyright 1991 by Council for Learning Disabilities. Reprinted with permission.

Remember:

1. Eyes on the teacher or on work

2. Sitting in seat
   Facing forward
   Feet on floor or legs crossed

3. Using correct materials

4. Working silently

Figure 6.4. Self-monitoring instructional sheet. *Note.* From "Using Self-Monitoring to Increase Independence," by D. K. Dunlap, G. Dunlap, L. K. Koegel, and R. L. Koegel, 1991, *Teaching Exceptional Children, 23*(3), p. 21. Copyright 1991 by the Council for Exceptional Children. Reprinted with permission.

Self-instruction or *self-talk* represents another potentially useful intervention. A variety of strategies are subsumed within this concept. Pfiffner and Barkley (1990) provide a good description of components of a self-instructional program:

> Self instructions include defining and understanding the task or problem, planning a general strategy to approach the problem, focusing attention on the task, selecting an answer or solution, and evaluating performance. In the case of a successful performance, self-reinforcement (usually in the form of a positive self-statement, such as "I really did a good job") is provided. In the case of an unsuccessful performance, a coping statement is made (e.g., "Next time I'll do better if I slow down") and errors are corrected. At first, an adult trainer typically models the self-instructions while performing a task. The child then performs the same task while the trainer provides the self-instructions. Next, the child performs the task while self-instructing aloud. These overt verbalizations are then faded to covert self-instructions. Reinforcement (e.g., praise, tokens, toys) is typically provided to the child for following the procedure as well as selecting correct solutions. (p. 525)

Self-instruction strategies that are clear and simple represent appropriate starting places for students who are ADHD. Such approaches, taught and practiced in the relevant environment (e.g., the classroom), likely will enhance the probability of success. Pfiffner and Barkley (1990, p. 529) recommend the STAR program, in which "children learn to *Stop, Think* ahead about what they have to do, *Act* or do the requested task while talking to themselves about the task, and *Review* their results."

Learning Strategies

The development of cognitive strategies such as self-talk in students provides a basis for the extension of cognitive interventions into training in the use of learning strategies. The use of learning strategies for students with attentional and learning problems has become extremely popular in the 1980s and into the 1990s. The growth in popularity and usage is clearly driven by the fact that a learning-strategies approach emphasizes independence for students. Central to its definition is the assumption that learning strategies focus on "learning to learn" rather than just on narrowly defined content topics.

The Council for Exceptional Children (1992) recommended that, since students with ADHD would be likely to have problems initially learning and then using learning strategies, the following instructional considerations be given:

> (a) isolating techniques that may be necessary for certain tasks; (b) demonstrating them or modeling them for the child; (c) having the child rehearse the strategies; (d) providing the child with feedback; and (e) encouraging and monitoring the child the first few times he or she uses the strategy in actual practice. (p. 23)

It is helpful to consider an explicit set of steps, consistent with the above principles, that can be followed in teaching strategies. The model developed by Deshler, Ellis, and Lenz (1996) is particularly apt (see Table 6.1).

A number of specific learning strategies have been developed that may be helpful to assist students with ADHD in regulating their own academic performance. three examples, covering variant academic concerns, include COPS, CRUSH, and SOLVE-IT. The overlap with study skills is clear with the last of these three.

The COPS strategy (Schumaker et al., 1981) is an error-monitoring strategy for writing. The acronym stands for four tasks within this strategy: capitalization, overall appearance (e.g., neatness, appropriate margins), punctuation, and spelling. With this strategy, students are taught to review their initial drafts of papers with specific attention to those four types of errors. The strategy has proven effective for use with students with learning and attentional problems, particularly at the upper elementary, middle, and secondary school levels (Shannon & Polloway, 1993).

CRUSH is a strategy for identifying unknown words in text (Polloway & Patton, 1997). The purpose of the strategy is to provide the reader with a system for using existing word-analysis skills in figuring out words as they appear. The assumption of the strategy is to encourage the students to use the least intrusive strategy (i.e., the one that least interferes with reading comprehension) when they encounter an unknown word in text. The steps include the following: C—use context clues or contextual analysis to make an educated guess as to what the word is; R—rapidly review key graphic features of the word (e.g., initial consonants, prefixes, suffixes) for further clues;

Table 6.1
Stages of Acquisition and Generalization

Stage	Phase
1. Pretest and commitments	1. Orientation and pretest
	2. Awareness and commitment
2. Description of strategy	1. Orientation and overview
	2. Current strategy and remembering system
3. Modeling of strategy	1. Orientation
	2. Presentation
	3. Student enlistment
4. Verbal elaboration and rehearsal	1. Verbal elaboration
	2. Verbal rehearsal
5. Controlled practice and feedback	1. Orientation and overview
	2. Guided practice
	3. Independent practice
6. Advanced practice and feedback	1. Orientation and overview
	2. Guided practice
	3. Independent practice
7. Confirmation of acquisition, generalization commitments	1. Confirmation and celebration
	2. Forecast and commitment to generalization
8. Generalization	1. Orientation
	2. Activation
	3. Adaptation
	4. Maintenance

Note. From *Teaching Adolescents with Learning Disabilities: Strategies and Methods* (p. 38), by D. D. Deshler, E. S. Ellis, and B. K. Lenz, 1996, Denver: Love Publishing. Copyright 1996 by Love Publishing. Reprinted with permission.

U—if the word is <u>u</u>nimportant to the meaning of the passage (e.g., a proper name), it does not need to be analyzed and can be skipped over; S—if a word requires more <u>s</u>ystematic analysis, the student will need to break the word into syllables and use phonetic analysis skills to read it; and, H—seek <u>h</u>elp from external sources (e.g., teacher, dictionary).

SOLVE-IT is a strategy for solving problems in mathematics. This strategy provides students with a systematic approach to the steps required for finding solutions to word problems. The steps are as follows: S—<u>s</u>ay the problem to yourself, since being able to repeat the problem is prerequisite to being able to solve it; O—<u>o</u>mit any unnecessary pieces of information and numbers that are not central to problem solution (i.e., problem distractors); L—<u>l</u>isten for words that provide clues to the mathematical operations to be performed; V—change the written <u>v</u>ocabulary words into math numbers and symbols; E—write a mathematics <u>e</u>quation; I—<u>i</u>ndicate the appropriate answer to the equation; and, T—<u>t</u>ransfer the numerical answer back to the context of the problem (Polloway & Patton, 1997).

Study Skills and Organizational Tactics

Many learning strategies, including some of those discussed above, can also be considered to be study and organizational skills. For example, to the extent to which successful editing in writing is important to effective study, the COPS strategy helps to promote the necessary independence that is the goal for students with attentional and related learning problems.

Study skills represent an "invisible" curriculum. Although they are admired as important accomplishments for all students, and increasingly at the secondary and postsecondary levels, they are rarely directly taught. While many normally achieving students manage to develop a reasonably effective approach to study and organization in the absence of direct instruction, it is safe to conclude that students with attentional and related learning and behavioral problems will need instruction on specific skills in this area. There is little question that these skills are critical for the achievement of independence.

Multipass (Schumaker, Deshler, Alley, & Denton, 1982) is a reading comprehension and study strategy derived from the traditional

SQ3R (Survey-Question-Read-Recite-Review) strategy. Multipass refers to the fact that students can be taught to make three passes through reading material. The *survey* pass has the student review, among other things, the title, any bold headings, and the summary or conclusion. The *size-up* pass directs students to review the comprehension questions at the end of the chapter. The *sort-out* pass provides an activity that enables students to organize the information in the chapter for response.

A particularly effective way to promote successful study skills is through the use of advanced organizers. Advanced organizers include any strategy provided to students prior to or along with content to be learned that will facilitate its retention and understanding. Most advanced organizers have a visual-pictorial component that facilitates learning. Figure 6.5 provides an example of an advanced organizer developed by Ellis (1993) that facilitates the learning of content information. Figures 6.6 and 6.7 provide advanced organizers for use in writing expository text structures (Englert & Mariage, 1991).

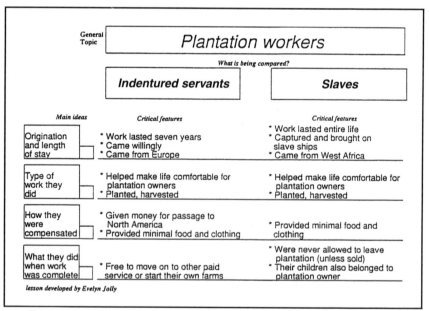

Figure 6.5. Content advanced organizer. *Note.* From "Integrative Strategy Instruction: A Potential Model for Teaching Content Area Subjects to Adolescents with Learning Disabilities," by E. Ellis, 1993, *Journal of Learning Disabilities, 26,* p. 375. Copyright 1993 by PRO-ED, Inc. Reprinted with permission.

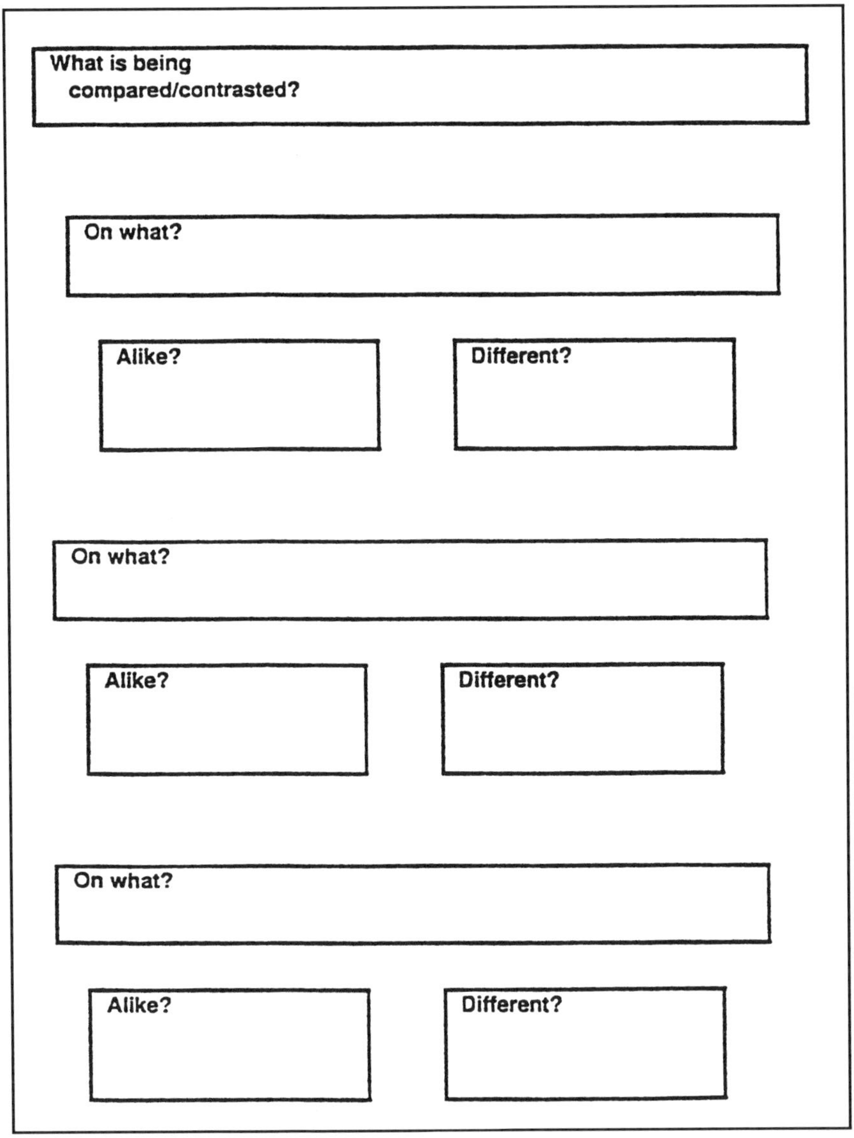

What is being compared/contrasted?

On what?

Alike?

Different?

On what?

Alike?

Different?

On what?

Alike?

Different?

Figure 6.6. Expository text structure: Compare/contrast. *Note.* From "Shared Understandings: Structuring the Writing Experience through Dialogue," by C. S. Englert and T. V. Mariage, 1991, *Journal of Learning Disabilities, 24*, p. 333. Copyright 1991 by PRO-ED, Inc. Reprinted with permission.

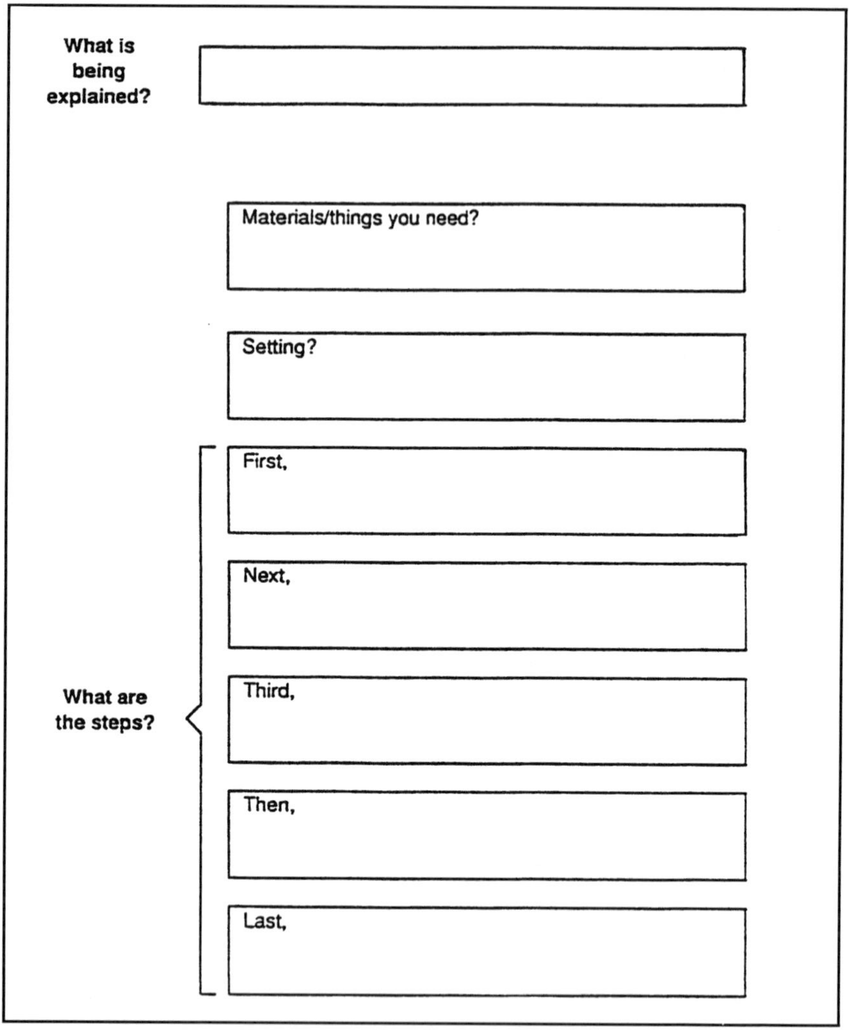

Figure 6.7. Expository text structure: Explanation. *Note.* From "Shared Understandings: Structuring the Writing Experience through Dialogue," by C. S. Englert and T. V. Mariage, 1991, *Journal of Learning Disabilities, 24,* p. 333. Copyright 1991 by PRO-ED, Inc. Reprinted with permission.

Advanced organizers can take numerous forms. The key element is that they provide students with a structure that assists them in understanding the concepts to be learned and retaining the information. Although advanced organizers are often provided by teachers (e.g., in the simplest form, a lecture outline), when the structure is shared with students and they are taught to use it, they can become excellent student-regulated strategies. The two examples of expository text structures (see Figures 6.6 and 6.7) are particularly good examples of this type of organizer.

Social Skills

Instructional programs for students with attentional and learning problems cannot be limited to academic interventions. Rather, many students will also have need for interventions that focus on the development of social skills, especially given the fact that about half of all children with ADHD have peer-relation problems (Guevremont, 1993). While self-management and learning-strategy approaches are clearly sufficiently flexible to also accommodate an emphasis on the acquisition of social skills, strategies for social skills are nevertheless discussed separately because of their critical importance to peer relations and postsecondary adjustment. Interventions that hold particular promise for students with attention-deficit/hyperactivity disorder are discussed below.

Guevremont (1993, pp. 6–7) identifies the following goals for social-skills training for children with ADHD:

- provide successful peer contacts
- increase knowledge about appropriate behavior and adaptive social skills
- promote successful peer interactions in the natural environment
- alter the child's social status within the peer group

In order to achieve these goals, training programs should be developed that promote self-regulation and offer frequent opportunities for practice and self-monitoring.

Goldstein and Goldstein (1990) outline a social-skills training program that includes skills taught across six training sessions. The structure is as follows (pp. 342–343):

Session I
- listening
- meeting people—introducing self, introducing others

- beginning a conversation
- listening during a conversation
- ending a conversation
- joining an ongoing activity

Session II

- asking questions appropriately
- asking favors appropriately
- seeking help from peers
- seeking help from adults
- following directions

Session III

- sharing
- interpreting body language
- playing a game successfully

Session IV

- suggesting an activity to others
- working cooperatively
- offering help

Session V

- saying thank you
- giving a compliment
- accepting a compliment
- rewarding self

Session VI

- apologizing
- understanding the impact of one's behavior on others
- understanding others' behavior

Final Thoughts

- Cognitive interventions are important strategies to consider for use with children with ADHD.
- Caution should be used with interventions that have not been validated with the ADHD population.
- Self-management includes varied techniques such as self-assessment, self-instruction, and self-monitoring.
- Self-monitoring is an intervention that has been used successfully with students with varying disabilities and attentional problems.
- Learning strategies include approaches that teach students how to learn and control their own learning.
- Specific examples of learning strategies include COPS, CRUSH, and SOLVE-IT.
- Study and organizational skills represent an important curricular area for students who are ADHD.
- Social-skills training programs provide explicit instruction for individuals who do not acquire social competence via typical human interactions and indirect instruction.

CHAPTER 7

Understanding the Use of Medications

Medical personnel are getting more and more involved in providing interventions to children and adolescents with attention deficits and hyperactivity. The history of ADHD actually has a medical basis. During the 1950s and 1960s, some children were identified as having minimal brain injury or minimal brain dysfunction. Typical characteristics of those children included attention deficits and hyperactivity. The mere fact that those children were labeled with terms that suggested organic brain damage resulted in a medical model of treatment, including the use of drug therapy, for many of them. Also, during that period, schools were providing minimal special education services for children with such problems, leaving a void of services that was filled with medical interventions.

Many different interventions have proven effective with children with ADHD, including those with a medical basis. However, the mere presence of attention problems and hyperactivity should not result in a decision to intervene medically. That decision should come only after a great deal of thought has been given to the variety of possible interventions. The decision to use medical treatment will depend on several factors, but primarily on the degree of the child's impairment in academics, social skills, and other areas (Herskowitz & Rosman, 1982). Children whose impairments in those areas are minimal are less likely to need medication than those whose impairments are so severe that they result in major disruptions (Smith, Polloway, Patton, & Dowdy, 1995).

Although not always necessary, a popular method of helping children with ADHD control their behaviors and attention is medical therapy. The estimate of the number of school-age children receiving medication to help in controlling behavior and attention problems is 5.96%

for elementary students, 3.86% for middle school students, and 0.4% for high school students (Safer & Krager, 1988). Those numbers have increased dramatically over the past twenty years. Although there is no one accepted explanation, some possible reasons for the widespread increase in the use of medication include the following:

- Medication is an easy way to control many students' behaviors and attention.

- More families and physicians are aware of ADHD and the potential for medical intervention.

- More children are being identified as having ADHD, for whatever reason.

- Research has demonstrated the effectiveness of some medications to control students' behaviors and attention.

- Many schools are doing an ineffective job of helping students with ADHD achieve success.

Regardless of the reason, the fact is that more and more school-age children and adolescents are receiving behavior control medications. As a result, teachers and other school personnel must have a basic understanding of the different types of medication used, possible negative side effects of those medications, and their specific role with medical intervention.

How Medication Works with ADHD Children

Medication therapy for children with ADHD can be defined as treatment by chemical substances that prevent or reduce inappropriate behaviors, hopefully resulting in academic and social gains for children with learning and behavior problems. The exact reason certain medications have a positive effect on hyperactivity, attention deficits, and academic success is not understood; however, as early as the 1930s Bradley (1937) noted that some children who experienced attention deficits and hyperactivity responded positively to stimulant medication. He observed that "when taking stimulant medication, the students in his school spent more time on their schoolwork and less time arguing and fighting among themselves . . ." (Gadow, 1993, p. 53).

And, in 1940, Bradley and Bowen found that stimulant medication actually resulted in improved academic performance by some students. Regardless of the potential impact of those findings, it was not until the 1970s, when the success of children in school—especially children who were experiencing various types of disabilities—became a national issue, that the findings began to receive attention among educators and parents.

While it is not understood exactly how or why various chemicals impact on attention, hyperactivity, and learning, several different outcomes have been found to result from such medications (Smith, Finn, & Dowdy, 1993). These include *desired outcomes, no desired effect,* and *side effects.* Table 7.1 summarizes these outcomes. The use of these medications is intended to result in a desired outcome, which for most of these children is increased attention on task and reduced inappropriate behaviors. These desired outcomes, in turn, frequently lead to improved academic and social achievement by allowing the child to attend to learning tasks and act appropriately in social situations.

While desired outcomes are the obvious reason for placing students with ADHD on medication, some medications, with some children, result in no apparent desired effect. In such situations, the desired effects do not materialize either because the medication is not

Table 7.1
Possible Outcomes to Medication

Positive	No Effect	Negative
• increased attention		• weight loss
• improved schoolwork		• irritability
		• behavior swings
• improved social skills		
		• nausea
• increased appropriate behaviors		
		• damage to organs
• decreased inappropriate behaviors		• precipitation of Tourette's syndrome
		• dizziness

in the proper dosage, or because the medication simply does not work on a particular child. Changing the dosage level or trying a different medication may result in the desired effects. A third possible result from medical intervention is side effects, or changes that are not desired. Examples are drowsiness, nausea, and skin reactions (Howe, Harris, & Tarantino, 1992). Figure 7.1 lists some possible negative side effects. Side effects must be monitored by medical professionals, family members, and school personnel to prevent any major problems resulting from the medication. Specific side effects for various drugs will be discussed later. In most instances, when the medication is stopped, the side effects subside.

The first large-scale studies that investigated the effects of stimulant medication on children with attention deficits and hyperactivity were completed by Abikoff, Gittelman, and Klein (1980) and Abikoff and Gittelman (1985). In several studies including large numbers of students in New York, it was determined that children receiving methylphenidate both increased their time on-task with school work and decreased their motor-activity levels. The improvement was so significant in some cases that the children with attention deficits and hyperactivity were indistinguishable from their classroom peers (Abikoff, Gittelman, & Klein, 1980; Abikoff & Gittelman, 1985). While the scientific reasons for such positive results from medical interventions were not understood, the results were overwhelming enough to result in more studies and an increased use of medical intervention with children who were experiencing ADHD.

Possible Negative Side Effects

- nausea
- dizziness
- weight gain
- weight loss
- irritability
- damage to internal organs

- skin rash
- precipitation of Tourette's syndrome
- mood swings
- growth deficiencies

Figure 7.1. Possible negative side effects.

Medications Used to Control ADHD

Numerous different medications are effective in controlling attention deficits and hyperactivity. Medications are labeled using both a generic name and a trade or brand name. The generic name reflects no involvement of a commercial company in the marketing of that particular medication, while the trade or brand name, on the other hand, indicates that a particular company is manufacturing and marketing the medication. The symbol ® to the right of the medication's name indicates that the manufacturer has registered the name, which is then restricted to use by that manufacturer.

The primary medications used with children who display attention deficits and hyperactivity include:

- methylphenidate (generic)

- amphetamines (class of drugs)

- pemoline (generic)

- trycyclic antidepressants (class of drugs)

- antipsychotics (class of drugs)

- Clonidine® (trade)

- lithium (generic)

- carbamazepine (generic)

Of all these medications, methylphenidate is by far the most commonly used. Studies have revealed that as many as 84% to 93% of medical professionals who prescribe medication for children with ADHD select methylphenidate (Copeland et al., 1987; Safer & Krager, 1988).

Methylphenidate

Teachers and parents frequently speak of children being on Ritalin®, which is the brand name for methylphenidate. Ritalin can be described as "a mild central nervous system (CNS) stimulant, available as tablets of 5, 10, and 20 mg for oral administration" (*Physician's Desk Reference*, 1994, p. 835). The typical initial dosage of Ritalin is 5 mg, two to three times daily; this can be increased according to weight or observed need after the initial adjustment period (Herskowitz & Rosman, 1982). Students who display marked anxiety, tension, and agitation should not be given Ritalin. Also, the medication should not be used with children who have glaucoma, motor tics, or a family history or diagnosis of Tourette's syndrome (*Physician's Desk Reference*, 1994).

Benefits of Methylphenidate

Methylphenidate has been shown to result in improvements in many different areas, including social skills (Whalen et al., 1987), self-esteem (Kelly, 1990), and academic performance (Douglas, Barr, O'Neil, & Britton, 1988; Ullmann & Sleator, 1985). These benefits generally result from increased attention to tasks, as well as a decrease in motor activity levels. Table 7.2 summarizes the positive effects of methylphenidate on various academic tasks.

Side Effects of Methylphenidate

Although methylphenidate has been proven effective in helping children control their hyperactivity and inattentiveness, some negative

Table 7.2
Effects of Methylphenidate on Various Academic Tasks

Authors	Findings
Connors (1972)	Improvement in a number of academic areas
Douglas et al. (1986)	Reading improvement
Kupietz et al. (1988)	Reading improvement
Murray (1987)	Schoolwork not impacted
Pelham et al. (1985)	More effect on arithmetic than reading
Richardson et al. (1987)	Improved academic performance related to improved attention and on-task time
Richardson et al. (1988)	Positive effect on reading scores
Wallander et al. (1987)	Improvement in overall school behaviors

Note. Developed from *Managing Attention Disorders in Children,* by S. Goldstein and M. Goldstein, 1990, New York: John Wiley.

side effects can result from taking this medication. Family members and school personnel must be aware of these side effects and alert medical personnel should they become problematic. Some of the possible side effects include:

- nervousness
- insomnia
- hypersensitivity
- anorexia

- nausea
- dizziness
- headaches
- weight loss

For the most part, these side effects abate with a decrease in dosage or a temporary cessation of the medication. However, they are generally considered acceptable considering the effectiveness of the medication on hyperactivity and attention problems and the resulting benefits (Goldstein & Goldstein, 1990). Table 7.3 describes precautions to using this drug.

Pemoline

Pemoline can be described as a central nervous system stimulant that is dissimilar to methylphenidate and other amphetamines. It is principally sold under the brand name of Cylert® (*Physician's Desk Reference,* 1994). The typical initial dosage of pemoline is 18.75 mg each morning, going to 75 mg per day in a single dosage for ongoing treatment (Herskowitz & Rosman, 1982). Studies of pemoline have resulted in findings similar to those of other stimulants on children with attention deficits and hyperactivity, including less motor activity, improved social skills, improved attention to tasks, improved intellectual functioning (Dykman, McGrew, & Ackerman, 1974) and improvement with hyperactivity (Connors, 1972). These findings make the medication a good choice for many children with attention problems and hyperactivity.

A major concern with this drug is its possible negative effect on liver function. Therefore, pemoline should not be used with children who have known hepatic disorders (*Physician's Desk Reference,* 1994). Other negative reactions that family members and school personnel should be aware of and monitor include:

- convulsive seizures
- hallucinations

Table 7.3
Precautions When Using Ritalin

Drug dependence	• Ritalin should be given cautiously to individuals with a history of emotional problems and drug or alcohol dependency.
	• Individuals with problems may increase their dosage on their own to a level that can lead to a psychic dependence.
	• Careful observation during drug decreases should be made to detect any signs of depression.
Usage during pregnancy	• The effect of Ritalin during pregnancy has not been established; therefore, prescription of Ritalin to women of child-bearing age should be limited.
Adverse reactions	• Nervousness and insomnia are the most common adverse reactions, usually controlled by reducing the dosage.
	• Other reactions may include hypersensitivity, including skin rash, anorexia, nausea, dizziness, blood pressure and pulse changes, abdominal pain, and weight loss.

Note. From *Physician's Desk Reference,* 1994, Oravell, NJ: Medical Economics Company.

- precipitation of Tourette's syndrome
- weight loss
- nausea and stomachache
- growth retardation
- skin rash

For the most part, negative side effects decrease after initial treatment. However, if symptoms persist, dosage should be reduced or discontinued (*Physician's Desk Reference,* 1994); the negative side effects then generally disappear.

Amphetamines

Amphetamines are a class of medications that result in stimulation. Amphetamines are often called "uppers" or "speed." For children with attention deficits and hyperactivity, many different amphetamines have an apparent opposite effect; for the most part, they reduce hyperactivity and assist students in attending to specific activities. Dextroamphetamine® is a commonly used amphetamine for children with these conditions. It is the only stimulant approved for children under the age of six years. Although "not recommended" for children between the ages of three and six years, there is a treatment schedule (Goldstein & Goldstein, 1990). For older children, the initial dosage is generally 2.5 mg, two to three times daily, adjusted according to body weight and observed need. It is available in 5 and 10 mg tablets (Herskowitz & Rosman, 1982).

Like other medications used with children who are experiencing hyperactivity and attention deficits, dextroamphetamine is a legally controlled substance. Amphetamines, as a general group of drugs, have been abused extensively. As a result, school personnel must be alert to any inappropriate use of these drugs. School personnel should also be aware that after prolonged high dosages of amphetamines, sudden cessation can result in extreme fatigue and mental depression (*Physician's Desk Reference,* 1994).

Another commonly used amphetamine is obetrol. Obetrol is used with children with ADHD but should not be used with individuals who are experiencing hypertension, hyperthyroidism, glaucoma, or cardiovascular disease; it has been shown to exacerbate these conditions. Other adverse reactions to amphetamines may include cardiovascular palpitations, increased blood pressure, restlessness, dizziness, insomnia, tremor, headache, and exacerbation of motor tics or Tourette's syndrome (*Physician's Desk Reference,* 1994). School personnel should be alert to all of these possible side effects and report them to family members, as well as the school nurse.

Trycyclic Antidepressants

Several trycyclic antidepressants are occasionally used with children with ADHD. A common one is imipramine, marketed as Tofranil® which is often used with children who for a variety of reasons cannot take stimulants. It is believed to act on neurotransmitters in the brain (Rief, 1993). The general initial dosage of imipramine is 10 mg, twice daily. This is increased to 20 to 100 mg per day in later stages of treatment (Herskowitz & Rosman, 1982).

Tofranil should not be given to individuals with a history of cardiac problems. General adverse reactions to the medication may include confusion, insomnia, anxiety, restlessness, and tremors. The drug can also cause skin rashes, diarrhea, and nausea (*Physician's Desk Reference*, 1994).

Antipsychotics

Although not used frequently with children who are experiencing ADHD, antipsychotics are occasionally prescribed for this group to counteract hyperactivity and attention problems. There are many different antipsychotics; the ones most likely used with children with ADHD are Mellaril and Thorazine. Mellaril is effective in reducing excitement, hypermotility, agitation, and tension. It is considered appropriate for children who are exhibiting severe behavior problems marked by combativeness or explosiveness (*Physician's Desk Reference*, 1994). Thorazine has also been shown effective in treating children with severe behavior problems, hyperactivity, and attention problems. The regular initial dosage for both Mellaril and Thorazine is 10 mg twice daily; for maintenance 20 mg daily or more is common (Herskowitz & Rosman, 1982).

Mellaril and Thorazine may cause several negative reactions, including:

- drowsiness
- jaundice
- cardiovascular problems
- central nervous system disorders
- allergic reactions (*Physician's Desk Reference*, 1994)

As with other types of medication for children with ADHD, these drugs should be monitored closely by family members, educators, and medical personnel.

Clonidine

Clonidine is a drug that may be given to children with ADHD that acts very differently than stimulants or antidepressants. Often prescribed for adults with hypertension, it has also been shown to reduce symptoms associated with ADHD (Rief, 1993). Reported adverse reactions to clonidine are minimal and generally decline over a period of time. Some possible reactions include dryness of mouth, drowsiness, and localized skin reactions (*Physician's Desk Reference*, 1994).

Lithium

Still another drug given to children with ADHD is lithium, which is also often prescribed for manic-depressive illness; continued use of lithium may diminish manic episodes. It is not recommended for children under twelve years of age (*Physician's Desk Reference*, 1994). The usual initial dosage of lithium is 150 mg, three times daily, with later dosage ranging between 450 and 1,200 mg per day (Herskowitz & Rosman, 1982).

Lithium can result in a variety of negative side effects, including hand tremor, mild thirst, nausea, diarrhea, vomiting, drowsiness, muscular weakness, and lack of coordination. As with other medications, many of these reactions may subside after continued use of the drug or after a brief lapse in treatment (*Physician's Desk Reference*, 1994).

Carbamazepine

Marketed with the brand name Tegretol, carbamazepine is an anticonvulsant that has been shown to be effective in treating complex partial and grand mal seizures. Caution should be observed with carbamazepine. Dizziness, drowsiness, and unsteadiness, nausea, and vomiting are the most common reactions after initial treatment. More serious reactions may affect the hemopoietic system, skin, and cardiovascular system. The nervous, respiratory, and digestive systems may also be affected (*Physician's Desk Reference*, 1994).

Role of School Personnel in Medical Interventions

Although school personnel may see their role as limited when a child is receiving medical interventions, it is critical that they remain closely involved with the entire treatment program. There are many different roles for school personnel to play with children who receive medication. These include:

- team member

- parent educator

- monitor

- reporter

The first role for school personnel is that of a team member. Medical intervention should never be provided in a vacuum. Rather, it should only be a component of the total treatment program. Behavior management, academic modifications and accommodations in the classroom, and environmental modifications should all be included in the total treatment program (Smith et al., 1995). While some children may respond very well to these types of interventions, others may need the addition of medical intervention to enable them to improve their success in academic and social settings. Teachers and other school personnel are integral components of the therapeutic team that must be involved in such diverse treatment methods (Rief, 1993).

Teachers should also serve as parent educators. They should ensure that parents understand the likely positive and negative effects of medications. While teachers may not be the professionals who provide this information, they should work closely with medical personnel, including school nurses, to ensure that family members get this information. Conferences with parents, such as the IEP conference, would be an ideal opportunity for school personnel to ensure that family members understand the medication their child is receiving. They especially need to be sensitive to the short-term negative side effects that could occur, including weight loss, irritability, and disruption of normal sleep habits (Goldstein & Goldstein, 1990).

An extremely important role for teachers to play when working with a student who is taking medication for attention problems and hyperactivity is that of monitor. Teachers must monitor the child for improvements as well as for the development of side effects that should be brought to the attention of family members and medical personnel. In order to do this effectively, school personnel must become knowledgeable about the various medications used by children. They should consult the school nurse, or even the child's physician in some cases, to obtain information that will enable them to better understand the likely and possible reactions to the medications being used.

Once school personnel have adequate knowledge about a particular medication, they should develop a mechanism that will help them monitor the child's behaviors and report observations to the child's parents. There are two types of symptoms that teachers should be aware of when making their observations. Objective symptoms are things that teachers can detect through direct observation of a student's behaviors. Lethargy, irritability, and agitation are examples of objective symptoms. Subjective symptoms are things that school personnel have to ask students about; they are not directly observable. For example, a teacher would have to ask a student if he had a stomachache or was feeling nauseated (Howe, Harris, & Tarantino, 1992). Although not as apparent as objective symptoms, subjective symptoms are just as important for teachers to note.

Monitoring children on medication is one of the most important things school personnel can do as part of a medical intervention strategy. There are several cautions and responsibilities for school personnel when observing children who are receiving medication. These include (Howe et al., 1992):

- Because school personnel are the closest adults to students a large part of the day, they are responsible for observing, recording, and describing symptoms to family members and health care providers.

- Both objective and subjective symptoms should be included in observations.

- Family members and health care providers will likely rely heavily on the report developed by school personnel; therefore, the observations must be accurate and recorded.

- Measuring and recording observations are a critical component for school personnel.

Although any routine monitoring plan will serve this purpose, it is recommended that school personnel develop a form that will provide structure to observations of the child. Different forms have been developed by school personnel to accomplish this task. Figure 7.2 includes an example of a monitoring form that could be used. The key in any monitoring form is to provide enough structure for the teacher or other school personnel to record specific observations over a specified

---

Daily Medication Monitoring Form

Student's Name _____

Student's Grade _____   Teacher _____

Medication _____   Dosage _____

Administration Schedule _____

Date of Observation _____   Person Observing _____

Time	Observable Behaviors	Student Complaints

Form given to _____ on _____
      Person receiving report   Date

Figure 7.2. Medication monitoring form.

period of time. Regardless of the intentions of the school personnel, without such a mechanism, observations will be forgotten or not even made.

The final role for school personnel is reporting. The frequency with which school personnel record and report their observations will vary. For example, school personnel should pay a great deal more attention to observing and reporting when medication is first started or when dosages change. Of course, in order for school personnel to know to attend more to their observations and reporting, parents must inform them that there has been a medication change. When medication is first being tried on a student, school personnel should closely observe the child and report their observations daily to the case manager, physician, or parent, as designated. After the medical regimen has been established, weekly or monthly reporting is sufficient. If medication is changed, or if the dosage level is varied, observations and reporting should once again be made daily. The chart in Table 7.4 provides a guideline for observing and reporting observations to family members.

One role that teachers and other school personnel should never play in the area of medication for students with ADHD is that of decision maker or judge. Most parents contemplate a great deal before agreeing to place their children on medication. This decision must be made by parents, with the assistance of medical professionals (Rief, 1993). All school personnel should do when parents are deliberating about this issue is to provide as much valid information as possible for them to consider. Again, this information in no way should present a biased opinion about medication and ADHD. Rather, it should be information that will assist parents in making the right decision for their children. And once the decision is made, school personnel must provide support for the student and family members and participate actively in the intervention team.

Final Thoughts

This chapter has presented information about medical intervention for children with attention problems and hyperactivity. The following points summarize the chapter:

- ADHD was initially a medically diagnosed disability.

(Continues on p. 171)

Table 7.4
Side Effects Checklist: Stimulants

Child_____ Date Checked_____

Person Completing Form_____ Relationship to Child _____

I. Side Effects

Directions: Please check any behaviors that this child exhibits while receiving his or her stimulant medication. If a child exhibits one or more of the behaviors below, please rate the extent to which you perceive the behavior to be a problem using the scale below (1=Mild to 7=Severe).

	Mild					Severe	
1. Loss of appetite	1	2	3	4	5	6	7
2. Stomachaches	1	2	3	4	5	6	7
3. Headaches	1	2	3	4	5	6	7
4. Tics (vocal or motor)	1	2	3	4	5	6	7
5. Extreme mood changes	1	2	3	4	5	6	7
6. Cognitively sluggish or disoriented	1	2	3	4	5	6	7
7. Excessive irritability	1	2	3	4	5	6	7
8. Excessive nervousness	1	2	3	4	5	6	7
9. Decreased social interactions	1	2	3	4	5	6	7
10. Unusual or bizarre behavior	1	2	3	4	5	6	7
11. Excessive activity level	1	2	3	4	5	6	7
12. Light picking of fingertips	1	2	3	4	5	6	7
13. Lip licking	1	2	3	4	5	6	7

II. Psychosocial Concerns

Please address any concerns you have about this child's adjustment to medication (e.g., physical, social, emotional changes; attitudes toward the medication, etc.).

III. Other Concerns

If you have any other concerns about this child's medication (e.g., administration problems, dosage concerns), please comment below.

Table 7.4 (Continued)

IV. Parent Concerns (for parents only)

Using the same scale above, please check any behaviors that this child exhibits while at home.

	Mild						Severe
1. Insomnia; sleeplessness	1	2	3	4	5	6	7
2. Possible rebound effects (excessive hyperactivity, impulsivity, inattention)	1	2	3	4	5	6	7

Note. From unpublished manuscript by L. A. Worthington, 1995, Birmingham, AL: University of Alabama at Birmingham. Used with permission.

- All children with ADHD should not be placed on medication.
- The degree of impairment is a key factor in determining if medication is warranted.
- Medication has been growing rapidly as a treatment method for children with ADHD.
- The exact way medication works to decrease hyperactivity and increase attention is not understood.
- Studies, beginning as early as the 1930s, showed the benefits of certain medications on children with ADHD.
- Drugs can have expected outcomes, no apparent outcomes, or side effects.
- Methylphenidate, sold as Ritalin, is the most commonly prescribed medication for children with ADHD.
- Many different drugs have been used effectively with children with ADHD.
- Most drugs have some negative side effects that should be noted.
- Most negative side effects will abate if the dosage is decreased or the medication is stopped.
- The most important role for school personnel is that of observer and reporter.

- School personnel should be considered an integral part of the medical intervention team.

- School personnel should use a structured form for their observations and reporting purposes.

- School personnel should always be informed by parents about the medication that a child is receiving.

- School personnel should be aware of the possible side effects that may result from a particular medication.

- School personnel should report their observations to family members and medical personnel on a regular schedule.

CHAPTER 8

Success through Collaboration

Co-Authored by
Kathleen McConnell Fad

The 1990s have witnessed a phenomenal increase in the commitment toward collaboration within the schools, in terms of the connections being developed between parents and families and teachers and school administrators, and between school and community agency personnel. This trend toward collaboration is particularly significant for students with attentional problems. Given the fact that problems with attention and related learning and behavioral domains most commonly are observed across living and learning settings, it becomes readily apparent that efforts toward collaboration are essential for maximizing the success of these students.

Home-School Collaboration

Professionals working with students who have attentional problems must begin their commitment to collaborative efforts with an appreciation of the challenges faced by parents and families who are raising a child who is ADHD. Reeve (1990, p. 77) drew a detailed picture of the challenges that such parents face when he related the following:

> Parenthood in the best of situations is a trying, humbling experience. Stress levels reach the breaking point from time to time in every family. For families with an ADHD child, the road is rougher. ADHD children are not as reinforcing to parents as are other children—they are harder to love, and they exert constant pressure. Parents must exercise constant supervision. At home, the ADHD child's room typically is messy and disorganized; getting dressed and ready for school often requires direct help, and may degenerate into a battle;

structured situations such as mealtimes can be disastrous; and family outings may turn into embarrassing fiascos at any time. Peer interactions have to be monitored, and sometimes contrived, due to the child's unpopularity. Homework may not be completed in a reasonable time period, or at all, without regular supervision. Yet the child looks typical and seems intelligent. Perhaps it would be easier to accept the behavior if the underlying problem were more evident.

It appears a safe assumption that when school personnel can establish good working relationships with parents and families, the school experiences of the children are enhanced. Thus an important objective for the schools should be to achieve and maintain such relationships. Most professionals acknowledge the importance in general of parent and family involvement in the schooling of their children, and this importance can be especially critical for students with attentional problems. However, for programs that promote home-school collaboration to be truly effective, the goal must be more than just, for example, the students' classroom success. Winton (1986) cautioned that while the value of this involvement has been documented extensively, much of what school personnel have done with parents has been related to their children's goals (i.e., student progress), with less attention given to parental outcomes (i.e., their particular needs). Both can be critical elements of parent involvement efforts in comprehensive programs for students with attentional problems. Teachers and parents (and other family members) gain from cooperative relationships that truly flow in both directions and are concerned with success in home and school settings.

While the case for the importance of strong school-home relationships on behalf of children with ADHD seems to be without detractors, it is interesting to note that research confirmation has trailed this assumption. For example, the literature review reported by Fiore, Becker, and Nero (1993) indicates that no empirical research had been reported that was specifically designed to evaluate the implementation or promotion of home-school collaborative efforts. Rather, the researchers indicate that the limited database that does exist concerns largely clinically based intervention. The studies in this database unfortunately appear to have limited direct application to interactions of school personnel with parents and family members.

Although the empirical base for home-school collaboration is only now beginning to evolve specifically in the area of attention-deficit/hyperactivity disorder, it nevertheless seems reasonable to rely on the attention that has been given to such collaboration for students with disabilities in general. Clearly the focus of that work underscores the fact that systematic attempts to involve parents in collaborative efforts have major advantages for enhancing school programs.

Positive Interactions

It is critical that home-school collaborations be built on positive interactions. To achieve this goal, professionals need to consider the types of needs that parents and families may have as well as the vehicles available for communication and collaboration.

In terms of the parents' potential needs, it is of no surprise that these can be many and varied. Reeve (1990) highlighted a number of them, including clear and accurate information on their child's problem; the opportunity for open and frequent communication; access to counseling support or professional assistance in behavior management; and assistance in making connections with other parents for mutual support. Perhaps the overriding need of parents from teachers and other school professionals is the belief that meeting the child's needs is truly a shared concern and that input from family members will be respected.

What vehicles are available to facilitate communication? Polloway, Patton, Payne, and Payne (1989) have outlined a series of home-school interactions that can be used to promote successful collaboration. These are discussed in the following paragraphs.

Conferences

All teachers are regularly involved in parent conferences, which can provide an important opportunity to demonstrate understanding of the unique home situations experienced by families with a child with attentional problems. Turnbull and Turnbull (1986) stress that when involved in conferences, teachers need to be able to reinforce parental comments, paraphrase what has been said, respond appropriately to parental affect and feelings, question effectively, and summarize the major points brought up. In short, teachers must engage in active listening and must be clear communicators.

Conferences may be of three relatively distinct types (Polloway et al., 1989). *Procedural conferences* relate to student assessment and program planning and review. IEP meetings for students who have been identified as disabled and who receive special services are one example. *Crisis conferences* arise in response to a current, acute problem and can be initiated by either the parent or the teacher. They are characterized typically by a need for immediate action. *Routine conferences* occur throughout the year on a scheduled or unscheduled basis and may be formal or informal. Routine meetings, when not driven by regulatory requirements or crises, provide an excellent opportunity for both parents and teachers to build positive relationships—this is particularly critical in the case of children with challenging attentional and behavioral problems.

Polloway and colleagues (1989) offer the following general guidelines that may be helpful with conferences:

- Be honest and direct.

- Avoid technical terms and concepts that parents may not understand.

- Be clear and concise.

- Do not speculate about issues for which you have no information. Discuss only what you know and what you can document.

- Prepare for the conference by notifying parents well in advance, organizing your notes, reviewing pertinent information, planning an agenda (for more formal meetings), and creating a pleasant environment.

- During the conference, create a positive atmosphere, set the purpose of the meeting, have student work samples available, take notes of what is being discussed, and end the meeting with a positive comment.

- After the conference organize your notes for future reference, initiate action on any items requiring attention, and determine when a followup meeting is necessary. (pp. 143–144)

Written Communication

A second common form of interaction, written communication, can range from a simple note to a more formal report. Particularly important are progress reports. Often, these occur only at the end of a grading period; however, more regular correspondence about progress would be valuable. For some students who are ADHD this communication may need to be daily; for others it can occur less frequently. Regardless of schedule, teachers should develop systems that facilitate the ongoing sharing of progress information. For example, student assignment books with space for homework assignments—and for teacher and parent comments as well—may be a simple yet effective form of interchange that can easily occur daily.

Telephone Communication

The third communication mechanism is the telephone, obviously used by teachers and parents alike for sharing information, usually of a more immediate nature. Some teachers encourage parents to call them at home, while others discourage this practice. Particularly in the case of a child with significant learning and behavioral problems, a teacher's job can be enriched by open lines of communication with parents, sometimes requiring availability beyond the school day.

Documentation of every telephone conversation with parents that pertains is particularly important. These notes not only provide an ongoing perspective for a particular situation but also can be invaluable if questions arise about a specific intervention or program at a later date.

Home-School Programming Concerns

Two general areas provide important foci for home-school collaboration: homework and behavior management. The general concerns of those areas and unique reports for students with ADHD are discussed below.

Homework

An important area that must be addressed within the spectrum of possible home-school collaboration issues arising around the child with ADHD is that of homework. As Epstein, Polloway, Foley, and Patton (1993) note, concerns about homework have escalated since the mid-1980s as an outgrowth of the series of national reports that were critical of the American educational system (e.g., National Coalition of Advocates for Students, 1985; National Commission on Excellence in Education, 1983). One central concern of such reports was that the standards were too low in American schools and that, among other things, students consequently spent substantially less time on homework than did their peers from other nations (National Commission on Excellence in Education, 1983; Turvey, 1986). These reports commonly called for an increased commitment in this area. For example, the Forum of Educational Organizational Leaders (Strother, 1984) recommended that teachers minimally require one hour of homework daily from students in elementary school and at least two hours from high school students. These calls have not gone unheeded. The reaction was almost instantaneous; the National Assessment of Educational Progress (NAEP) report (U.S. Department of Education, 1990) found that by 1988, students of all ages were being assigned more homework than they had been four years earlier. More recently, this trend has been confirmed in research on school policies (Roderique, Polloway, Cumblad, Epstein, & Bursuck, 1994) and classroom practices (Polloway, Epstein, Bursuck, Jayanthi, & Cumblad, 1994).

As the trend toward an increased commitment to homework in general education grows, it clearly creates practical concerns for students who have attentional and learning problems, especially since they most often are educated in regular classrooms. It can be anticipated that homework would be particularly problematic for these students for several specific reasons, including:

- Homework tasks are often quite mundane and rarely provide the novelty or excitement that might help to focus a child's attention and increase his or her motivation.

- Other competing stimuli (e.g., television, radio) are generally present in the home and may distract attention from homework tasks.

- Feedback for homework is typically delayed until at least the next day and, in some class situations, may be virtually nonexistent beyond credit or failure for completion.

- Consequences for homework assignments may be unclear to students in general and to the student with ADHD in particular, and thus the assignments and the process may fail to afford the requisite level of incentive.

As a consequence of these common problems associated with homework, several probable critical needs are likely to exist, including:

- the need for additional supervision and/or assistance by parents or older siblings in the home;

- the necessity of more powerful consequences than may come from the satisfaction of simply achieving completion;

- the need for more frequent and immediate feedback both in the home and in the classroom.

A variety of responses to the possible problems experienced in homework have been suggested in the literature. In their review, Roderique and colleagues (1994) highlight the following areas:

- assessment of possible homework problem areas as a basis for designing specific intervention efforts (see Anesko & O'Leary, 1982);

- prescriptive, individualized programming targeting specific problems and/or providing general assistance in learning strategies and study and organizational skills (see Chapter 5);

- increasing the relevance of the assignment by relating it to areas of student interest, life skills, and, in the case of those in special classes, general education content;

- assigning homework that actually can be completed on an independent basis, thus with emphasis on proficiency or maintenance-type activities;

- controlling the time that assignments may take to assure that completion is realistic;

- providing for the evaluation of homework papers and direct feedback to students on aspects of specific assignments;

- providing sufficient guidance when assignments are made.

Home-School Management Programs

A second major area of home-school programming is the development of collaborative management programs. For many parents and families who have a child with ADHD, the schools provide an important resource in designing effective interventions that go beyond the psychopharmacological alternatives that were discussed earlier.

Teachers can give assistance to parents for behavioral management in the home. The guidelines for such interventions are simply outgrowths of the principles for effective management, which were discussed earlier in Chapter 4. Particularly cogent to the development of programs that will be helpful to parents are interventions that have been discussed and evaluated by both parties. Possible options include positive reinforcement programs such as contingency contracts and token economies. For example, Figure 8.1 presents a record-keeping device that can be used in home token programs. Token systems can be taught to parents, who can then follow through with their implementation.

The student's success with the school curriculum and his or her behavior in the school are also areas of concern. One way of addressing these concerns with parents and families involves the establishment of home-school contingencies. Home-school contingencies can be highly effective and also cost efficient and hence should be among the first interventions to be considered in managing the in-school behavior of a student with attentional problems (Pfiffner & Barkley, 1990). Such interventions typically include providing reinforcement contingencies in the home based on the documentation of learning and behavioral reports from school.

Home Token Program

NAME____________________ WEEK OF________________

TARGET BEHAVIORS TO EARN POINTS	POINT VALUE	POINTS EARNED EACH DAY						
		MON	TUE	WED	THU	FRI	SAT	SUN
TOTAL POINTS								

____________________ = _____ **Points**
____________________ = _____ **Points**
____________________ = _____ **Points**

Figure 8.1. Home token program: Record keeping. *Note.* From *The ADD Hyperactivity Workbook for Parents, Teachers, and Kids* (p. 100), by H. G. Parker, 1988, Plantation, FL: Impact Publications. Copyright 1988 by Impact Publications. Reprinted with permission.

The basic mechanism for home-school contingencies is written notes, often formally designed based on a structure that highlights a student's behavior vis-à-vis an identified target or targets.

Polloway and Patton (1993) highlight two possible interventions that facilitate such communication: daily report cards and passports. These two interventions are similar and can be relatively easily used to enhance communication and consistency within a home-school management program.

Daily report cards (see Figures 8.2 and 8.3) present a first option that is potentially very useful for providing feedback to parents as well as providing a structure for a rich menu of reinforcers to be delivered in the home. As Dougherty and Dougherty (1977) note, such reports can be used for feedback on schoolwork, homework, and behavior. Report cards can range in complexity from forms calling for responses to simple rating scales to more precisely designed behavioral instruments with formal definitions and the designation of direct, daily behavioral

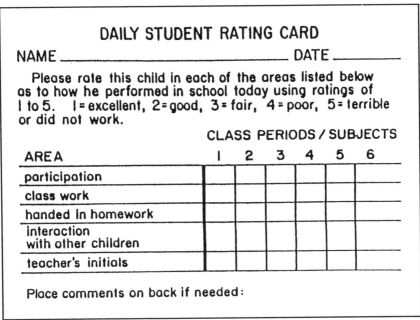

Figure 8.2. Daily report card: Used with home token system. *Note.* From "Educational Placement and Classroom Management," by L. Pfiffner and R. Barkley, 1990, in *Attention Deficit Hyperactivity Disorder: A Handbook for Diagnosis and Treatment* (p. 522). New York: Guilford. Copyright 1990 by Guilford. Reprinted with permission.

Daily Report Card: Controlling Aggressive Behavior

Name _____ Date _____

Please evaluate this child in the following areas of behavior during free or unstructured school time, especially during *recess*. Using a rating of 1 = excellent, 2 = good, 3 = fair, 4 = poor, please place a number beside each behavior listed below for each recess or free-time period this child is observed each day.

Free Time/Recess

	#1	#2	#3	#4
1. Keeps hands to self; does not push, shove, pinch, or touch others wrongly	☐	☐	☐	☐
2. Does not fight with other children (hitting, kicking, biting) or try to provoke them by tripping them, shoving them, or taking their things	☐	☐	☐	☐
3. Follows rules	☐	☐	☐	☐
4. Tries to get along well with other children	☐	☐	☐	☐

Other comments:

_____

_____

_____

Figure 8.3. Daily report card: Controlling aggressive behavior. *Note.* From "Educational Placement and Classroom Management," by L. Pfiffner and R. Barkley, 1990, in *Attention Deficit Hyperactivity Disorder: A Handbook for Diagnosis and Treatment* (p. 522). New York: Guilford. Copyright 1990 by Guilford. Reprinted with permission.

measures. Further, they can be tied to nonspecific consequences sub-sequently to be determined by parents and child or to stated specific short- and long-term reinforcement.

The *passport* is another communication tool between home and school. Passports typically take the form of notebooks that students bring to each of their classes and then take home daily. Individual teachers (or all of a student's teachers) and parents can make regular notations. Reinforcement is based on carrying the passport in addition to the specific target behaviors that are indicated on it (Runge, Walker, & Shea, 1975; Walker & Shea, 1988).

Home-school contingencies offer excellent options for teachers concerned about the management of classroom behavior of students who have ADHD. Pfiffner and Barkley (1990, p. 521) comment further on ways to effect the creation of programs that enhance student performance:

> The success for a program requires a clear, consistent system for translating teacher reports into consequences at home. Some programs involve rewards alone; others incorporate both positive and negative consequences. Some studies suggest that a combination of positive and negative consequences may be more effective than rewards alone. However, in cases where parents tend to be overly coercive or abusive, reward-only programs are preferable.

School Collaboration

A second critical area of collaboration is *within* the school environment. The majority of students who have ADHD will be in general education classrooms for most of their school day. Their successful performance and achievement will depend in part on the effectiveness of collaborative efforts among general and special education teachers, counselors, and others. Effective collaboration must: 1) facilitate communication among personnel, 2) establish and maintain positive working relationships among members of the team, and 3) successfully solve problems to meet the challenging educational needs that students with ADHD demonstrate. The first prerequisite for effective collaboration is a commitment to change, since a collaborative, cooperative model is different from more traditional service delivery models in schools.

Commitment to Change

Because collaboration and teamwork have not been the norm for teachers, moving to this type of service delivery model will require a strong commitment on the part of everyone. Bauwens and Hourcade (1995, pp. 7–8) have described some essential requirements for educational collaborators, including their willingness to:

- comprehensively evaluate themselves and the present system;

- discard many old practices and procedures that are nonfunctional or irrelevant for contemporary education programs; and

- actively seek out or develop, implement, and evaluate new and more effective procedures.

Changes of any kind may be uncomfortable, frustrating, and difficult. When change involves actual practices in schools, a shift from comfortable routines can seem overwhelming.

Collaboration requires that people share ideas, resources, time, responsibility, money, and materials. It also requires a level of trust and respect if changes are to be substantive.

It is important to recognize that there are barriers to collaboration. The types of barriers include:

- *attitudinal barriers,* including fear of losing power, abandonment of long-held traditions, and cynicism about proposed innovations;

- *structural barriers* like administrative support problems, legal regulations, excessive paperwork, and time issues involving scheduling and workload allocation; and

- *competency barriers,* including lack of knowledge and lack of skills, especially when general educators have not been adequately prepared to deal with students who have special needs (Bauwens & Hourcade, 1995).

Recognition of the barriers and resulting efforts to overcome them may be the first priority of collaborative teams.

Who Should Collaborate?

The members of collaborative teams can (and should) vary, depending on the goals of the collaboration, the student who is the focus of the program, and the type of solutions considered. When collaboration is for prereferral problem solving, team members often include an administrator, a special education teacher or consultant, the student's general education teacher, and a counselor. For students with ADHD whose problems have resulted in modifications under Section 504 or the Vocational Rehabilitation Act of 1973, or who have been identified in the special education category "Other Health Impaired" under the IDEA, team members may also include a psychologist or psychological associate, a behavior specialist, a social worker, and the school nurse or physician.

Facilitating Communication

Schools are busy places. One of the most difficult problems faced by teachers, administrators, and counselors is communicating effectively. Educators are constantly responsible for supervising and guiding students; consequently, they often have little free time. Teachers also spend much of their time in classrooms that physically isolate them from each other. While it is imperative that special and regular education teachers and others communicate effectively, it can be a challenge.

One of the first tasks for professionals who want to collaborate in school is to structure the communication process. This entails finding ways to communicate frequently and efficiently. Some communication will be face-to-face communication in one-to-one or group meetings; other communication will be written or via the telephone or computer network.

Regardless of the nature of the communication, everyone on the school team must make it a priority, so that misunderstandings are kept to a minimum and positive interactions are maximized. Dealing with students who have ADHD is challenging (and sometimes exhausting). Since their behavior can fluctuate widely in a short period of time, it is important for educators to be consistent and united in their efforts at remediation. Otherwise, students with ADHD may take advantage of inconsistencies, fail to meet established criteria, and set up situations in which one professional feels left out or at a disadvantage.

One of the most common ways that the communication process is put into place is through a referral from a general or special education teacher. Teachers who have students with ADHD in their classes often need strategies for helping those students get organized, limiting their movement, dealing with their behavioral difficulties, and accommodating their learning problems. Many school districts have developed quick and easy referral forms that teachers can use to request assistance from a consultant or from a problem-solving team.

Some examples of simple referral forms and response forms are presented here. Figure 8.4 is a simple referral that is intended to be copied onto brightly colored 3x5 index cards, which teachers can then place in the consultant's or team leader's mailbox. Figure 8.5 is a reply form from a consultation model in the Northside Independent School District in San Antonio (Autry, Cotton, and Dockendorf, 1994). Figure 8.6, from the STAND (Students Taking a New Direction) program, can be used by an intervention team as they consider the student with ADHD. It takes into account current problems, strengths of the student, and possible strategies (Fad, 1993). Many collaborative programs like the two mentioned here now serve students with a variety of behavioral and academic needs, including an increasing population

---

Consultation Request

Please stop by at my conference/planning period on
_____ at _____.
(date)   (time)

I would like to discuss _____.

_____   _____
(teacher)   (today's date)

Figure 8.4. Consultation request. *Note.* From *STAND: Students Taking a New Direction (Information Packet)*, by K. M. Fad, 1993. Unpublished manuscript. Copyright 1993 by author. Reprinted with permission.

identified with ADHD. Using simple forms like these can streamline communication among professionals. The response to students with ADHD who experience difficulties can be quick and easy, perhaps preventing serious problems that require more intensive interventions.

I received the referral you

sent on _____

today. I will be dropping

by on _____

about _____ o'clock.

If this is not a convenient

time please call and we

will reschedule.

Thank you!

Figure 8.5. Reply form. *Note.* From *Northside Independent School District Behavior Consultation Model Manual,* by M. Peters, 1996, unpublished manuscript. Reprinted with permission.

STAND Referral Form

Date_____ Student's name _____

Grade_____ Teacher's name_____

Sp ed or Reg ed?_____ Parents contacted? _____

Reasons for referral: _____

_____

_____

 Positive qualities/strengths of student: _____

_____

Health problems?_____

_____

Other agencies involved? _____

Strategies suggested: _____

_____

_____   _____
          STAND consultant   Teacher's name

Next meeting date: _____

───

Date: _____

Committee decision: _____

_____

_____   _____   _____
STAND consultant   Principal   Teacher

Figure 8.6. STAND referral form. *Note.* From *STAND: Students Taking a New Direction (Information Packet),* by K. M. Fad, 1993. Unpublished manuscript. Copyright 1993 by author. Reprinted with permission.

Building Team Relationships: Spending Time Together

It is impossible to share concerns, ideas, resources, or solutions to problems without working together face to face; nevertheless, finding adequate, common planning time for team members remains a troublesome barrier to effective collaboration. There are several ways that the logistical problems pertaining to planning time can be solved. These include:

- scheduling flexible staff development days;
- scheduling regular student assemblies that are monitored by administrators or volunteers, freeing teachers for collaborative activities;
- using paraprofessionals for instruction and as teacher assistants;
- scheduling common daily lunch periods and common preparation periods;
- using year-round calendars that allow release time from direct instruction; and
- encouraging nonschool personnel to participate in education and provide student activities while educators meet to collaborate (Bauwens & Hourcade, 1995).

In order for school collaboration to be effective, administrators must make common planning and meeting time for team members a priority. Without it, teachers may end up feeling frustrated, isolated, and ineffective. Once the meetings have been arranged, the next task is to ensure that the time together is spent productively.

Successfully Solving Problems: Efficient Use of Time

Several models can assist teams in structuring their meetings for maximum productivity. Some guidelines for efficient use of meeting time include:

- setting and staying with an agenda;
- establishing priorities;
- setting time limits;
- limiting interruptions;

- starting and ending on time; and

- planning the next meeting.

One way to make good use of meetings is to follow a twenty-five-minute problem-solving model. This model requires team members to work toward a solution to a student's behavioral or academic problems by following a prescribed schedule. Since many problem-solving meetings never progress beyond the stage of describing the nature of the problem, using a time-limited model can greatly increase team effectiveness. When using this type of structure, it is advisable to select a team leader and a time keeper. The people assigned to these roles can vary, but during each session, it is important to adhere as closely as possible to the time allotted to each activity. Figure 8.7 presents the framework for implementing a twenty-five-minute problem-solving model.

Other useful tools can be found in *Collaboration in the Schools* by West, Idol, and Cannon (1989). The Problem-Solving Worksheet (Figure 8.8) and the Action Plan (Figure 8.9) are both useful guides when teams collaborate to formulate decisions about students' problems. Having forms available often helps team members stay focused on the task at hand and may prevent them from digressing or engaging in long, unproductive "gripe sessions."

Continuing the Collaboration Process

While implementing small changes is sometimes quick and easy, making substantive changes that last is more difficult. There are several long-term activities that teams must undertake if collaboration among all educators is to continue. First and foremost, educators must develop plans for effective, pertinent staff development. Teachers who are well informed and highly skilled will be both more comfortable and more effective with students whose ADHD requires modifications in the instructional style or the learning environment.

Another critical activity is support for the collaborative structures that have been developed. When new organizational structures are established, they must be supported with adequate resources. Administrators should take a key role in this process, ensuring that teachers have the materials, time, and personnel support necessary for students with ADHD to succeed.

25-Minute Problem-Solving Session for

_____

#1   Team members: _____   _____

                          _____   _____

#2   Define the problem (4 min.): _____

      _____

#3   Generate possible solutions (5 min.):

                          _____

                          _____

                          _____

#4   Select criteria for solutions (3 min.):

                          _____

                          _____

#5   Choose the first option (2 min.):

                          _____

#6   Decide on the action plan (6 min.)
      (who will do what, how, and when):

      _____

      _____

#7   Decide how and when to evaluate
      progress (3 min.):_____

      _____

#8   Choose the next date, time, and place to
      meet (2 min.).

Figure 8.7. Framework for 25-minute problem-solving model. _Note._ From _STAND: Students Taking a New Direction (Information Packet),_ by K. M. Fad, 1993. Unpublished manuscript. Copyright 1993 by author. Reprinted with permission.

Problem-Solving Worksheet

Resource teacher _____

Classroom/content teacher _____

Date _____

Problem: _____

_____

Details: _____

_____

Alternative Solutions	**Possible Consequences**	**Priority**
1. _____	_____	_____
_____	_____	
2. _____	_____	_____
_____	_____	
3. _____	_____	_____
_____	_____	
4. _____	_____	_____
_____	_____	
5. _____	_____	_____
_____	_____	
6. _____	_____	_____
_____	_____	
7. _____	_____	_____
_____	_____	
8. _____	_____	_____
_____	_____	

Solution to be tried first: _____

_____

Figure 8.8. Problem-solving worksheet. *Note.* From *Collaboration in the Schools,* by J. F. West, L. Idol, and G. Cannon, 1989, Austin, TX: PRO-ED, Inc. Copyright 1989 by PRO-ED, Inc. Reprinted with permission.

Action Plan

Implementation Steps	When	Who
_____	_____	_____
_____	_____	_____
_____	_____	_____
_____	_____	_____
_____	_____	_____
_____	_____	_____
_____	_____	_____
_____	_____	_____
_____	_____	_____
_____	_____	_____

How will the plan be monitored?

_____

_____

_____

_____

How will progress be evaluated?

_____

_____

_____

_____

_____

Date and Time of Next Appointment

_____

_____

Figure 8.9. Action plan. *Note.* From *Collaboration in the Schools,* by J. F. West, L. Idol, and G. Cannon, 1989, Austin, TX: PRO-ED, Inc. Copyright 1989 by PRO-ED, Inc. Reprinted with permission.

Finally, it is important that current, helpful information be disseminated to collaborative team members. The number of students identified with ADHD has grown significantly in recent years. Along with the increase in identified students has come an increase in information related to diagnostic procedures, medical interventions, therapeutic techniques, teaching strategies, and available curricular materials. Educators will benefit from access to information, but the materials disseminated must be prioritized, since time available to teachers is always in short supply.

Collaboration within schools seems to be increasing, as educators strive for ways to serve their diverse and challenging population of students. Although students with ADHD are commonly educated in general education classrooms, their educational needs often include modified, adapted, or restructured teaching techniques and materials. Collaboration is essential for their success.

Final Thoughts

- Collaboration is an important component of successful school programs.

- The benefits of home-school collaboration vis-à-vis students with ADHD have not been adequately researched but can be assumed to be potentially significant.

- Home-school interactions can be promoted through conferences, written communication, and telephone contacts.

- Programming options include effective homework programs and behavior-change interventions.

CHAPTER 9

The Transition to
Adult Living[1]

Planning for the future has long been recognized as a good idea. Interestingly, when efforts to plan for any student's future have been made, programmatic activities have traditionally focused on further education or employment, ignoring other areas in which competence will be needed (e.g., daily living and community skills).

Special education and related services have been mandated for a long enough time now so that we should be able to expect better outcomes for students who are eligible to receive them. Until rather recently, however, a key piece of the preparation-for-life puzzle had been overlooked. This missing piece involves the systematic consideration of what students with disabilities need to function successfully as adults. Essentially, if students have the knowledge, skills, services, and supports to deal effectively with the various demands of adulthood, then it is likely that their lives will be more enriched and satisfying.

Fundamental Concepts of Transition

All students acquire the knowledge and skills, or access the services and supports, required to meet everyday challenges in a number of

[1]Parts of this chapter are taken from "Transition and Students with Learning Disabilities: Creating Sound Futures," by G. Blalock and J.R. Patton, 1996, *Journal of Learning Disabilities, 29,* pp. 7–16. Reprinted with permission.

different ways. Families often are the source of much of what young adults will need to know; and students on their own pick up useful information and learn needed skills through incidental events. Schools should also be addressing many of the important demands of adulthood. However, none of these sources, singly or in combination, prepare youth as comprehensively as is needed.

Services that prepare students with special needs for adult life have been operative for quite some time in many locales. In the past, however, they may have been called something else and may not have focused on students with ADHD. Nevertheless, it is important to acknowledge that many special education teachers, guidance counselors, and other personnel were very much in the business of preparing students with special needs and their families for the realities of life after high school long before the current emphasis on transition commenced. It is also useful to note that many families, to whom much of the planning for the future has fallen, have also done a splendid job of getting their adolescent sons and daughters ready for the big show.

In 1994, the Division on Career Development and Transition (DCDT) of the Council for Exceptional Children adopted a new definition of transition that arguably is the best blend of contemporary thinking on this concept. Acknowledging that as students with special needs leave school they will have to assume various adult roles in the community, the definition promotes the notions that transition education starts in the beginning levels of schooling and that student involvement in this process should occur whenever possible. The DCDT definition reads as follows:

> Transition refers to a change in status from behaving primarily as a student to assuming emergent adult roles in the community. These roles include employment, participating in post-secondary education, maintaining a home, becoming appropriately involved in the community, and experiencing satisfactory personal and social relationships. The process of enhancing transition involves the participation and coordination of school programs, adult agency services, and natural supports within the community. The foundations for transition should be laid during the elementary and middle school years, guided by the broad concept of career development. Transition planning should begin no later than age 14, and students should be encouraged, to the

full extent of their capabilities, to assume a minimum amount of responsibility for such planning. (Halpern, 1994, p. 117)

The transition planning process is multifaceted, reflecting a complexity that requires: a) a thorough understanding of this process, b) knowledge of what must be done, and c) a variety of skills to implement needed transition activities successfully. The model in Figure 9.1 depicts the interrelated aspects of the transition process and suggests that the primary responsibility of transition efforts should be shared by the student, his or her parents or guardians, and the school; however, in reality, all three sources might not contribute to this process. It is essential that all efforts lead to the acquisition of skills, knowledge, services, and supports that enable the student to successfully deal with the demands of adulthood. Being reasonably successful in meeting the challenges of everyday living, whether at work, at home, in school, or in the community, can lead to personal fulfillment—an idea that relates closely to the concept of quality of life as discussed by Halpern (1993).

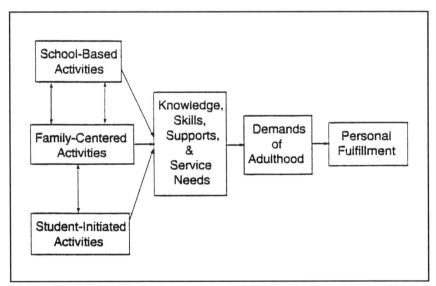

Figure 9.1. Elements of the transition process. *Note.* From *Transition from School to Adult Life for Students with Special Needs: Basic Concepts and Recommended Practices,* by J.R. Patton and C. Dunn, in press, Austin, TX: PRO-ED.

Transition Planning and Students with ADHD

The transition planning process provides just the opportunity needed to shape one's future in a powerful way. Adolescents and young adults can participate in and even manage the individualized transition planning process, supported by a multifaceted team. The team can guide students with ADHD in making and acting on their choices about further education, work, living arrangements, medical attention, physical and mental health supports, transportation options, leisure and recreation, and other life areas.

Blalock (1996) elaborates on the idea that the team should consist of the student, family member(s), critical teachers in special and general (especially vocational) education, an administrator or counselor, a postsecondary education representative, appropriate adult agency staff, and any others tied to essential transition services. Creative options for the future, and ways to achieve them, would be much more forthcoming in a group situation than if a single-service provider or student were making decisions alone. Team members can help each other stay future focused, targeting educational, vocational, and other critical goals after the student leaves high school (often three years or more in the future).

Cronin and Patton (1993) have helped students and educators envision potential postschool or transition goals by grasping the realm of adult life demands and then working backwards. Once the postschool goals have been agreed upon, the team must identify specific activities that will get the student moving toward accomplishing those goals. Many districts are finding that a one-page attachment to the IEP, or a section of the existing IEP form, works well for listing those activities; this serves as the individualized transition plan (ITP). Those particular objectives can then be translated into IEP annual goals and short-term objectives. By allowing the transition goals (or the ITP) to drive the instruction developed within the IEP, all involved parties (most important, the student and family) are clear about the overall focus, and content or skill acquisition is very connected to an outcome. An example of an ITP for a student with ADHD is shown in Figure 9.2.

The IEP/ITP requires that present levels of performance be documented, so that the team can identify where to start and what the critical areas of instruction are. This section, which should come early on the IEP form, provides the opportunity to set the tone of the planning

Individual Transition Plan

Student Profile

Darlene will be entering her final year of school in the fall. She has a long history of learning disability and attention-deficit/hyperactivity disorder. According to her guidance counselor, Darlene may not be receiving a regular high school diploma.

Darlene's mother has been supportive for the past 2 years; however, she has been absent many times before. As a result, Darlene is very independent and is determined to be as successful as possible. She is interested in working, perhaps in the transportation industry, as a driver. Darlene has a good attitude toward work and brings many assets to vocational and transition planning. Despite discouraging words from family and friends about her chosen career, Darlene is determined to succeed.

Individual Transition Plan

Student's Name __Darlene__
First   M.I.   Last

Birthdate _____   School _Eastland_____

Student's ID No. _____   ITP Conference Date _____

Participants

Name	Position
Darlene	student
Mary Susan	mother
Pat	special educator
Paul	vocational educator
Nina	classroom teacher

(Continues)

Figure 9.2 Individual transition plan. *Note.* From *Individual Transition Plans: The Teacher's Curriculum Guide for Helping Youth with Special Needs* (p. 145), by P. Wehman, 1995, Austin, TX: PRO-ED. Copyright 1995 by PRO-ED, Inc. Reprinted with permission.

Individual Transition Plan

I. Career and Economic Self-Sufficiency

1. Employment Goal	Darlene will be employed as a truck driver.
Level of present performance	Darlene has participated in 1 year of career exploration. Darlene has decided that she wants to be a truck driver.
Steps needed to accomplish goal	(1) Darlene and teacher will identify truck driving schools that have credibility and job placement; (2) mother will use community contact to help as well; and (3) student will serve as an intern at a moving company.
Date of completion	1/95
Person(s) responsible for implementation	classroom teacher, Darlene, and mother
2. Vocational Education/Training Goal	Darlene will participate in activities that allow practice on completing job applications, interviewing, using critical thinking skills, and obtaining a license to drive a truck.
Level of present performance	Darlene has decided to train as a heavy truck driver.
Steps needed to accomplish goal	(1) Darlene will practice completing job applications; (2) Darlene and vocational teacher will role play job interviewing skills; and (3) vocational and special educators will provide Darlene with necessary internship training experience.
Date of completion	6/95
Person(s) responsible for implementation	vocational educator, special educator, and Darlene
3. Postsecondary Education Goal	Darlene will enroll in one heavy truck driving academy.
Level of present performance	Darlene has expressed a strong interest in driving heavy trucks.

Figure 9.2. Continued.

Individual Transition Plan

Steps needed to accomplish goal	(1) Darlene will apply to truck driving academy; and (2) Darlene will meet with advisor from school to discuss job placement after training.
Date of completion	9/95
Person(s) responsible for implementation	Darlene
4. Financial/Income Needs Goal	Darlene will write and follow a monthly budget.
Level of present performance	Darlene has a part-time job.
Steps needed to accomplish goal	Darlene will purchase a spiral notebook. Darlene will list monthly expenses and demonstrate how to add and subtract expenses and income.
Date of completion	12/94
Person(s) responsible for implementation	Darlene

II. Community Integration and Participation

5. Independent Living Goal	Darlene will use the phone book to identify community resources.
Level of present performance	Darlene does not know how to use a phone book. She knows its purpose but has not demonstrated proficiency.
Steps needed to accomplish goal	Darlene will read through the index of the phone book. Darlene will practice looking up the names and telephone numbers of various agencies.
Date of completion	11/94
Person(s) responsible for implementation	teacher and Darlene

(Continues)

Figure 9.2. Continued.

Individual Transition Plan

6. Transportation/Mobility Goal	Darlene will be able to read road maps.
Level of present performance	Darlene has a driver's license and borrows the family car often.
Steps needed to accomplish goal	(1) Darlene will use sense of direction to locate north, south, east, and west; and (2) she will highlight route on map and will follow route and check landmarks.
Date of completion	6/95
Person(s) responsible for implementation	teacher and Darlene
7. Social Responsibility Goal	Darlene will take women's self-defense class at the YWCA.
Level of present performance	Darlene currently travels alone on many occasions.
Steps needed to accomplish goal	(1) Darlene will use phone book to locate phone number of the YWCA; (2) Darlene will call to get information; (3) she will enroll in self-defense class; and (4) she will evaluate skills as class progresses.
Date of completion	6/95
Person(s) responsible for implementation	Darlene, YWCA instructor
8. Recreation/Leisure Goal	Darlene will join the community volleyball team.
Level of present performance	Darlene has expressed an interest in participating in the activities at the Community Recreation Center.
Steps needed to accomplish goal	Darlene will sign up for team and will practice with team. Darlene will play as a member of the team.

Figure 9.2. Continued.

Individual Transition Plan

Date of completion	7/94
Person(s) responsible for implementation	Darlene and recreation instructor

III. Personal Competence

9. Health/Safety Goal	see Social Relationships Goal
Level of present performance	
Steps needed to accomplish goal	
Date of completion	
Person(s) responsible for implementation	

10. Self-Advocacy/Future Planning	N/A
Level of present performance	
Steps needed to accomplish goal	
Date of completion	
Person(s) responsible for implementation	

Student Career Preference

Work in the transportation industry

(Continues)

Figure 9.2. Continued.

Individual Transition Plan

Student's Major Transition Needs

1. _Vocational training_
2. _Postsecondary education at traveling academy_
3. _Reading road maps_
4. _Independent self-care and health management_
5. _Safety awareness_
6. _____
7. _____
8. _____
9. _____

Additional Notes

_____
_____
_____
_____
_____
_____
_____
_____
_____
_____
_____
_____
_____
_____

Figure 9.2. Continued.

process. Building on the student's abilities, rather than coming strictly from a deficit perspective, is much more in concert with transition planning. Students with learning disabilities will have numerous strengths among their various functioning areas of physical/motor development, social/behavioral performance, independent living skills, and career/vocational development. Stating those abilities provides the basis for effective outcome-oriented planning.

The Importance of Timing

In most cases, the development of a timeline for transition services has been a helpful framework to guide practitioners and researchers. The timeliness of various services (assessment, planning, instruction) is an element in the career development theories (aimed at the general population) of Donald Super, John Holland, and others. Specifically, opportunities for career awareness activities at the elementary level, career exploration at the middle school or junior high level, and career education at the high school and postsecondary levels are important for all students. They are particularly critical for students with learning disabilities whose incidental learning outcomes across their school careers may be spotty at best; systematic, focused instruction in life areas may be required for many of these students to be able to reach their educational and vocational goals. A suggested timeline for transition planning and its requisite elements for students with learning disabilities is presented in Table 9.1.

Critical Considerations in Transition Planning

IDEA mandates that students' interests and goals be considered as primary factors in transition decision making, a requirement that is long overdue for such critical life planning. In addition, key family members' visions, goals, and requests should drive decisions to an equal degree (Halloran, 1989); some states have even conferred families with agency status so that they can make decisions of the same weight as those of other agency representatives (Blalock et al., 1994). Differing wishes between the student and his or her family members may need to be resolved, compromised on, or even mediated, but the requests of both parties must be respectfully considered. Hopefully,

Table 9.1

Timelines for Transition Planning & Services for Students with ADHD

Preschool	Elementary	Mid-School	High School	Postsecondary
Developmental assessment	Academic, developmental, and informal interest surveys	Academic, adaptive, and interest assessments	9th—vocational interest, aptitude, & values 11–12th—update same Ongoing academic assessment	Formal vocational & academic
Individualized Family Services Plan (IFSP)	Individualized Education Program (IEP)	IEP, 4-year plan for high school	Individualized Transition Planning (ITP) as part of IEP	IEP/ITP and possible Indiv. Written Rehabilitation Plan (WRP) or other individual plans
Developmental and other curricula	Basic skills; work-related behaviors;[a] self-determination instruction; career awareness	Basic skills; work-related behaviors;[a] self-determination; career exploration	Basic skills (within functional context &/or college prep); self-determination; career education	Specific academic & vocational curricula
Chores at home	Chores, hobbies at home and in school	Rotated, varied small job tryouts, supervised experiences	Paid jobs (varied) with supervision gradually faded	Career entry placements

Note. From "Transition and Students with Learning Disability: Creating Sound Futures," by G. Blalock and J. R. Patton, 1996, *Journal of Learning Disabilities, 29,* p. 7–16.

[a]Work-related behaviors include social skills, work ethic, reasoning/problem-solving skills, punctuality, dependability, following through on

earlier training in self-determination and self-advocacy (particularly appropriate for students with learning disabilities) will have prepared the student to successfully negotiate decisions that are satisfactory to all. The need to begin such instruction (as well as instruction in the areas of work-related behaviors and career awareness and exploration) early on in school becomes evident when the demands at each age level are clarified.

Often, families will base requests, opinions, or comments on their own community or cultural values, accepted practices, or expected traditions. Linguistic differences introduce additional considerations. Rather than viewing these differences as problems, school and agency personnel are encouraged to consider language, culture, and exceptionality as gifts of diversity (Scott & Raborn, 1995); such a perspective matches the use of IEP/ITPs from a capacity-building rather than a deficit viewpoint. School and adult-agency personnel must critically review, and in most cases reject, any professional recommendations that are at odds with local mores or family wishes, unless the young adult knowingly and deliberately has chosen to act differently for his or her own perceived best interest. The professionals' role at that point may need to be gathering and collecting data to indicate potential outcomes of the chosen path(s) for both the student and the family.

Final Thoughts

The importance of comprehensive transition planning is underscored by the fact that the Individuals with Disabilities Education Act requires that a minimum level of transition planning be in place by the time a student is 16 years of age. This chapter has provided a brief introduction to the realities of transition planning for students with ADHD. The main points made in the chapter include the following:

- The focus of planning is on instructional (knowledge and skills) goals and linkage (supports and services) goals.
- Transition efforts should begin at the elementary level.
- Students should be active, competent participants in their transition planning.
- The transition planning process is a multifaceted process.

- The school, family, and student have a shared responsibility in preparing the individual for the challenges of adulthood.

- The transition team, in conjunction with the student, plays a key role in the transition process.

- Transition goals should be written as part of the IEP or may be included in an individualized transition plan (ITP), which some states require.

- It is critical to establish a time line for transition services.

- Students' interests and preferences should drive the transition planning process.

APPENDIX A

Guide to Classroom Intervention

Domain I: Attention/Impulsivity/Hyperactivity

Characteristics	Modifications
1. Exhibits excessive nonpurposeful movement (can't sit still, stay in seat)	Allow student to stand at times while working.
	Provide opportunity for breaks from sitting (e.g., run errands).
	Increase distance between desks.
	Build movement into activities.
	Seat student in quiet area.
2. Is easily distracted by auditory stimuli	Increase distance between desks.
	Pair oral instructions with written instructions.
	Cue student to stay on task (use a private signal).
	Allow student to use earplugs when completing assignment.
	Seat student in front of class.
	Utilize assistive technology during lectures/instruction (e.g., phonic ear system in which teacher speaks into a microphone while student is wearing earphones).

3. Is easily distracted by visual stimuli

Seat student in front of class.

Pair oral instructions with written instructions.

Seek to involve student in lesson presentation.

Cue student to stay on task using a private signal.

Seat student near "study buddy."

Break long assignments into smaller parts to coincide with span of attention.

4. Does not stay on task for appropriate periods of time

Assist student in setting short-term goals.

Give assignments one at a time to avoid "overload."

Instruct student in self-monitoring; may use a timer.

Cue student to stay on task using a private signal.

5. Has difficulty completing assignments

Seat student near good role model.

Seat student near "study buddy."

Break assignments into smaller parts so student can see an end to work.

Assist student in setting short-term goals.

Give assignments one at a time.

Reduce amount of homework.

Increase immediate rewards and consequences.

(Continues)

Characteristics

6. Verbally or physically interrupts conversations or activities

7. Loses place when reading orally

8. Sits and does nothing (daydreams)

Modifications

Attend to positive behavior with compliments, etc.

Set up behavior contract.

Instruct student in self-monitoring of behavior.

Praise student when hand is raised to answer question.

Seek to involve student in lesson preparation.

Set up social behavior goals with student and implement a reward program.

Prompt appropriate behavior with a private signal.

Utilize a bookmarker or template.

Enlarge reading material.

For book reports, etc., allow student to present material without reading it (develop cue cards with one main idea per card).

Avoid asking student to read orally.

Make student aware ahead of time what section he/she will be asked to read to allow for preparation/familiarity with material.

Cue student using a private signal (e.g., a touch to the shoulder).

Seat student near teacher.

Break long assignments into smaller parts and have student self-monitor using a timer.

9. Rushes through work with little regard for details (careless)

Reduce amount of homework.

Pair oral instructions and written instructions.

Seek to involve student in lesson presentation.

Allow extra time for task completion.

Allow student to stand at times while working.

Utilize self-check method (have a step-by-step checklist by which student can check work for error).

Remind student to check over work.

10. Does not pay attention to most important stimuli

Seat student near teacher.

Develop a private signal to prompt student to important stimuli.

Seat in distraction-reduced area.

Color-code or highlight material by degree of importance.

11. Shifts from one uncompleted activity to another

Break assignments into smaller parts.

Give assignments one at a time.

Be sure student has an uncluttered work area.

12. Does not appear to listen to what is being said

Pair oral instructions with written instructions.

Allow student to tape-record assignments and lectures.

Have student repeat important information in own words to ensure comprehension.

(Continues)

Characteristics	Modifications
13. Talks beyond appropriate limits	Cue student with private signal.
	Praise appropriate behavior.
	Set up social behavior goals with student and implement reward program.
	Prompt appropriate social behavior with private signal.
	Provide small-group social skills training.
14. Loses items needed for activities or tasks (e.g., paper, writing instrument, assignment)	Provide organization rules.
	Encourage student to have notebook with dividers and folders for work.
	Provide designated time each day for maintenance of organizational system.
	Develop checklist with student of necessary supplies for self-monitoring.
	Have student use homework assignment book.
	Regularly check desk or work area for neatness.
	Allow student to have an extra set of books at home.
	Use a briefcase with compartments for items.
15. Has difficulty working/playing quietly	Attend to positive behavior with compliments.
	Instruct student in self-monitoring of behavior.
	Provide small-group social skills training.

Domain II: Reasoning/Processing

Characteristics	Modifications
16. Makes poor decisions	Prioritize tasks and provide checklists while modeling the activity for student.
	Provide periodic monitoring of step completion and/or quality control.
	Build problem-solving experiences into curricula.
17. Makes frequent errors	Complete frequent performance checks.
	Teach self-check strategies (e.g., have a step-by-step checklist, ask student to check for errors).
	Select choice of activities to match student strengths.
	Provide counseling.
	Provide a peer support network.
18. Has trouble using previously learned information in a new situation	Utilize assistive technology (e.g., calculator).
	Employ mnemonic devices and memory strategies.
	Utilize peer mentors for periodic monitoring.
	Access counseling.
	Provide a peer support network.
	Provide multiple practice opportunities.
19. Has delayed verbal responses	Allow student to role-play with script to prepare for verbal interaction (e.g., IEP conferences, parent/teacher-student meetings).
	Have an advocate accompany student to meetings.

(Continues)

Characteristics

20. Takes longer to do a task than others

21. Has difficulty adjusting to changes (schedule, personnel, steps in a task, work conditions)

22. Requires more supervision than peers

Modifications

Educate school personnel and/or classmates to give student an opportunity to respond—this could occur through advocacy by self or others.

Shorten task.

Develop time lines and checklists to enable student to self-monitor.

Assign peer mentor to function as natural support.

Extend time limits.

Provide consistent schedule of daily assignments.

Provide clearly defined instructions.

Provide checklists of daily job tasks.

Thoroughly introduce and acquaint student with new staff and changes in scheduling.

Designate access to teacher's time.

Seat close to peer mentor or teacher.

Provide checklists of daily job tasks.

Provide audio or visual aids relating to specific tasks that student may consult when feeling the need for supervision.

Lengthen training period to allow student to gain strategies for self-monitoring.

23. Has difficulty getting started

Help the student identify and practice his/her preferred learning/processing style.

Gradually reduce supervision and frequency of feedback.

Provide/develop clearly defined organizational structure.

Provide/develop checklist of time frames.

Break tasks into small segments.

Provide/develop incentives for task initiation.

Utilize assistive technology (e.g., timers) to cue student to initiate task.

24. Has difficulty understanding social expectations

Increase awareness of socialization deficits and feelings of others through work with a drama coach.

Allow student to role-play social interactions.

Pair with peer or coach to act as social role model/mentor.

Provide group therapy.

Provide peer support group.

25. Requires concrete demonstrations

Provide ample "labs" for hands-on practice.

Utilize coach to provide extra time.

(Continues)

Characteristics

Modifications

"Walk through" or demonstrate each new task with student.

Conduct periodic assessment to be sure student has retained sequences for task completion.

Utilize assistive technology (e.g., videotapes of tasks that student can view when clarification is needed).

26. Requires extra practice

Provide a classroom setting that is flexible and allows extended time for completion.

Allow extended training periods.

Arrange for student to practice after hours (e.g., work with a tutor).

Utilize a peer mentor during learning periods to reduce anxiety.

Utilize assistive technology that student may access when extra practice is required (e.g., audio- and/or videotapes).

Provide guidance and counseling (school counselor).

Provide peer support group.

27. Has difficulty following oral instructions

Provide hands-on task demonstration.

Minimize auditory distractions.

Provide written or diagrammatic instructions.

Allow student to tape oral instructions, then take notes from tape.

28. Has difficulty following written instructions

Allow student to take notes when oral instructions are given, then ask teacher to check for completeness.

Provide a work sample that student may use as a model.

Utilize assistive technology.

Provide textbooks and other written materials, computer with scanner voice output, speaking Franklin language master, audiotape (e.g., recordings for the blind and dyslexic).

Provide someone to read written material aloud—peer or aide.

Provide oral instructions.

Provide hands-on demonstration.

29. Has difficulty following a map or diagram

Give instructions orally or in written format.

Allow student to tape instructions and play them back.

Place pictures of landmarks on enlarged map.

Provide hands-on task demonstration.

30. Is disoriented to time, place, purpose

Pair with a peer mentor or aide.

Teach student to use self-talk to stay focused.

Use watch with beeper.

Use frequent calendar checks.

Have students participate in goal setting.

(Continues)

Domain III: Memory

Characteristics	Modifications
31. Has difficulty answering questions regarding personal history	Develop a page of personal information that student may keep with him/her for quick reference.
	Develop and teach mnemonic strategies for remembering personal information.
32. Has difficulty repeating information recently heard	Provide/develop written instructions.
	Allow student to tape-record necessary information to play back as needed.
	Allow student to take notes from tape-recorded information.
33. Has difficulty repeating information recently read	Allow student to tape-record for multiple replay.
	Provide instructions orally, taped, or diagrammed.
	Utilize assistive technology: "Memo Mate."
	Utilize checklists.
34. Has difficulty retaining learned information	Arrange for student to maintain a notebook of work task steps and information.
	Utilize checklists of task steps.
	Pair with peer mentor to provide natural support.
	Be sure instructional process includes a review of recently learned material.
	Allow student to practice material to be retained by utilizing several modalities (visual, auditory, kinesthetic).
	Provide peer support group.

35. Has difficulty following multiple directions

Arrange for student to maintain a notebook of task steps and information.

Utilize checklists of task steps.

Allow student to tape-record instructions for replay as needed.

Break tasks/instructions into small segments.

36. Has difficulty performing tasks in correct sequence

Utilize checklists of sequential task steps.

Break tasks into small steps.

Utilize mnemonic strategies for remembering sequences of steps.

Utilize peer mentor or aide to cue and monitor.

37. Has trouble remembering such that daily activities are affected

Assist student in maintaining daily planner/calendar.

Develop "to do" checklists.

Utilize assistive technology to cue daily activities (e.g., timer, watch with timer, electronic planners).

Domain IV: Executive Function

Characteristics

Modifications

38. Has difficulty planning and organizing activities

Provide incentives for task initiation.

Prioritize tasks.

Provide written or auditory checklists.

Provide time frames.

Utilize assistive technology (e.g., watch with timer, computer with daily organization program, electronic calendar/organizer).

Utilize pocket calendar.

(Continues)

Characteristics	Modifications
39. Has time management difficulties (attendance, meeting deadlines)	Identify reason for difficulty (cannot tell time, transportation difficulties, personal problems that interfere with performance).
	Provide/develop checklists and/or written schedules for daily work.
	Reinforce each instance of appropriate behavior.
	Utilize assistive technology (e.g., watch with timer, computers with daily organization program, electronic calendar/organizer).
	Utilize pocket calendar.
	Utilize wall calendar.
	Teach student to project time requirements of steps.
	Use peer as natural support.
40. Has difficulty setting priorities	Build specific time into instructional program for:
	• direct instruction in setting priorities
	• practice in setting priorities
	• development of critical thinking skills
	• development of mnemonic technique for general prioritization.
	Check to be sure student has prioritized appropriately.
	Provide a list of prioritized tasks to student.

41.	Has difficulty attending to several stimuli at once	Place emphasis on most important stimuli.
		Model decision making in several settings.
42.	Has difficulty grasping complex situations	Provide explanations via the student's own processing strength (visual, auditory, haptic).
		Teach problem-solving strategies.
43.	Appears unaware of possible consequences of behavior and personal limitations	Provide role-play situations and model consequences; then have student describe the situation and consequences.
44.	Has difficulty inhibiting inappropriate responses	Provide a small-group or independent setting.
		Pair with a peer mentor or aide to provide visual cueing.
		Provide role-playing and other social skills training, to include videotaping.
		Provide counseling to clearly define appropriate response.
		Utilize self-advocacy strategies.
45.	Has difficulty sustaining appropriate behavior for prolonged periods	Reduce time required on task.
		Provide frequent breaks.
		Reward appropriate behavior.
		Have student critique video of own behavior.
		Provide peer role model.

(Continues)

Characteristics

46. Has difficulty generating strategies to solve a problem (social, academic, work)

47. Has difficulty monitoring own performance throughout activity (self-monitoring)

48. Has difficulty independently adjusting behavior (self-regulation)

49. Has difficulty identifying personal strengths and limitations

Modifications

Model thought processes during problem-solving examples.

Teach strategies (e.g., proofing work).

Provide feedback on inefficient strategies.

Identify buddy for collaboration.

Model thought processes during self-monitoring.

Use video for self-critiquing.

Use a peer for prompting.

Practice self-monitoring with feedback following.

Model thought processes for several situations.

Have student think of situations where he or she should have self-regulated or changed behavior.

Practice with counseling sessions following efforts.

Provide information from most recent assessment.

Have peers describe their own strengths and weaknesses.

Give concrete examples of strengths and limitations and discuss their impact in school or work settings.

Domain V: Interpersonal Skills

Characteristics	Modifications
50. Interacts inappropriately with teachers of same sex	Utilize conflict resolution strategies.
51. Interacts inappropriately with teachers of opposite sex	Utilize coaching services during initial phases of instruction.
	Provide role-play interactions.
	Provide social skills training.
52. Responds inappropriately to nonverbal cues	Teach identification of nonverbal cues.
	Provide careful education awareness to staff and classmates.
	Pair with a coach followed by peer mentor.
	Provide role-play interactions.
	Seat in close proximity to teacher.
	Establish a visual cue (signal) to alert student of behavior and allow for self-regulation (to cease the behavior).
53. Uses body language ineffectively	Provide careful education of disability awareness to staff and classmates.
	Have student role-play with videotaping.
	Provide/develop a specific cue (signal) to alert student to cease inappropriate behavior/action.

(Continues)

Characteristics

54. Uses eye contact ineffectively

55. Is verbally aggressive

56. Is physically aggressive

57. Is withdrawn; avoids social functions

58. Has difficulty accepting constructive criticism

Modifications

Provide social skills training; include videotaping.

Provide counseling related to self-esteem.

Have student restate assignments/requirements in own words to ensure understanding.

Assign to independent work station.

Utilize conflict resolution strategies.

Pair with peer model.

Reinforce decrease of verbal aggression.

Utilize anger management strategies.

Assign to independent work area.

Provide counseling.

Provide instruction in assertiveness training, social skills building, interview skills through role playing and videotaping.

Provide an LD Peer Support Group.

Pair with a peer mentor and provide small-group activities that match the student's strengths.

Provide extended training periods to ensure mastery of task processes.

Reinforce positive responses.

Provide frequent positive feedback.

Provide a correct work sample against which student can check and correct own work.

Provide peer support groups.

Have student role-play with an advocate prior to performance ratings.

Utilize positive self-task strategies.

Provide written task analysis of specific assignments.

Provide coaching followed by pairing with peer mentor.

Have designee periodically monitor performance of newly assigned tasks.

59. Has difficulty asking for help

Provide instruction in self-advocacy training, disability awareness, mock interactions with videotaping, positive self-talk strategies, coping with change.

Limit surprises and provide positive feedback.

Provide peer support group.

Pair with peer mentor to provide encouragement.

Start with simple tasks, gradually raising standard as confidence builds.

60. Exhibits signs of poor self-confidence

(Continues)

Domain VI: Emotional Maturity

Characteristics	Modifications
61. Displays inappropriate emotions for situation	Provide skills training that includes videotaping and role playing.
	Provide/develop a specific cue (signal) to alert student and allow for self-correction.
	Provide disability awareness education to staff and classmates.
62. Has difficulty accepting constructive criticism	Allow for extended training periods to ensure mastery of task process.
	Reinforce positive responses.
	Provide frequent positive feedback.
	Provide a correct work sample against which the student can check and correct own work.
63. Has difficulty asking for help	Provide written task analysis of specific assignments.
	Pair with peer mentor.
64. Exhibits signs of poor self-confidence	Provide self-advocacy training, disability awareness, mock interactions with videotaping, positive self-talk strategies.
	Provide peer support group.
	Pair with peer mentor to provide encouragement.

65. Displays inappropriate emotions for situation

Gradually share information relating to possible upcoming changes.

66. Has difficulty accepting new tasks without complaint

Start with simple tasks, gradually raising standard as confidence builds.

Have student talk with school counselor.

Pair with mentor.

Use job coach when new tasks are assigned.

Assign to independent work station.

Provide classroom education by advocate.

67. Is frequently upset, irritated

Identify peer to offer ongoing support.

Participate in counseling.

Modify demands.

Teach relaxation techniques and self-talk for calming.

Utilize relaxation tapes/techniques.

Play calming music in background.

68. Displays temper outbursts

Provide demonstrations of sequential task steps.

Provide social skills training.

Provide classroom education by advocate.

69. Is easily led by others

Utilize assistive technology to increase independence (e.g., watch beeper, timer).

Provide/develop checklists or time charts to include assigned tasks, time lines.

(Continues)

Characteristics

Modifications

Pair with peer who is conscientious as a mentor.

Provide classroom education by advocate.

Seat in an area separated from others.

Provide direct instruction to student to question the motives of others—he/she will not learn this from experience.

70. Appears unmotivated

Assign a conscientious peer to be mentor.

Provide model of accurate work sample student may use for comparison and self-correction.

Have student restate instructions to ensure understanding of expectations.

Provide direct instruction regarding task expectations in student's learning style.

Provide classroom education to ensure sensitivity to student's needs.

Provide peer support group or counseling to include esteem-building strategies.

Teach "teacher-pleasing" behaviors (e.g., sitting up straight, making eye contact with the teacher).

71. Does not follow classroom "rules"

Explicitly review rules on a periodic basis.

Have student restate rules in own words to ensure comprehension.

Have rules posted in chart form or have taped copy available for independent review.

Provide frequent and immediate positive feedback.

Utilize time management techniques.

Provide classroom education.

Pair with conscientious peer.

72. Has difficulty making and keeping friends

Provide sensitivity training and/or support groups.

Place in class or group that focuses on improving social skills.

Pair with a peer who displays excellent social skills as mentor.

Encourage student to participate in hobbies in the community as a basis for meeting people.

73. Displays a lack of awareness of social consequences of inappropriate interactions

Have student participate in social skills training in a group setting (videotaping counseling and role-playing).

Provide written and/or tape-recorded copy of all classroom rules and associated consequences.

Provide intermittent review of the social expectations of the classroom.

(Continues)

Characteristics

74. Has difficulty working in a group

75. Has difficulty working independently

76. Has tendency to overreact

Modifications

Provide earplugs to decrease distractions.

Provide work station separate from others.

Schedule job tasks that may be completed independently of others.

Provide social skills training and as student increases mastery, add to groups of increasingly larger size.

Pair with peer as mentor.

Have mentor prioritize tasks for individual.

Provide positive incentives for completed tasks.

Provide checklist of tasks to be completed.

Provide designated time for access to teacher for one-on-one instruction.

Provide group projects.

Teach/utilize conflict resolution strategies.

Develop strategies/plans to utilize natural support effectively.

Break job tasks into small units.

Allow frequent breaks.

Reinforce positive behavior.

Assign to independent work station.

Provide pharmacological therapy if ADHD or anxiety disorder has been diagnosed.

Domain VII: Coordination/Motor Function

Characteristics

77. Has difficulty performing gross-motor tasks (walking, sports, driving)

78. Has difficulty performing fine-motor tasks (writing, drawing)

79. Confuses left and right

80. Has difficulty keeping balance

81. Has slow reaction time

Modifications

Teach/utilize stress management strategies.

Have advocate educate classmates and teachers regarding disability-related characteristics.

Provide safety instruction with periodic monitoring.

Utilize assistive technology—allow written assignments to be typed.

Provide direct instruction.

Use special jewelry to designate (e.g., watch on left arm).

Provide direct instruction.

Teach self-advocacy.

Educate other students regarding problems.

Provide cueing by peer mentor, use assistive technology such as a timer.

(Continues)

82. Has limited endurance/stamina for motor activity

Break the day into smaller units of activity interspersed with sedentary tasks.

Plan breaks at appropriate times.

Build stamina slowly by increasing expectations.

Domain VIII: Communication

Characteristics

Modifications

83. Has difficulty understanding words

Utilize assistive technology (e.g., speaking language master, Franklin speller with dictionary).

Pair with peer to rephrase statements.

Provide written instructions in simple language.

Teach to ask for clarification.

84. Has difficulty learning new words

Utilize assistive technology (e.g., Franklin speller with dictionary).

Utilize dictionary and/or thesaurus.

85. Does not respond appropriately to information presented verbally (conversation, directions)

Provide instructions in written format.

Provide social skills training to focus on conversation.

86. Has difficulty communicating on the phone

Develop a "script" to outline ideas before using phone.

Utilize assistive technology (e.g., answering machine, e-mail, fax machine).

Assign a designee to make important phone contacts.

87. Fails to form speech sounds correctly

Allow written reports as opposed to oral communications.

Utilize self-advocacy strategies.

Provide peer support groups.

88. Substitutes one sound for another

Have student practice with a tape recorder.

Have student provide responses in written form.

89. Omits sounds

Have student practice with a tape recorder.

Have student provide responses in written form.

90. Substitutes words inappropriately

Utilize a "cue card" of words specific to subject.

Have student provide responses in written form.

91. Has word-finding difficulties

Utilize self-advocacy strategies.

Provide a peer support group.

Teach classroom survival words.

Utilize cue card of classroom survival words.

Select assignments that deemphasize oral communication.

92. Uses short, simple sentences

Teach vocabulary relevant to specific subject areas, then role-play to provide practical application.

Pair with peer who has good verbal skills.

Provide scripts to be read.

Teach sentence elaboration.

(Continues)

93. Has difficulty expressing ideas clearly

Utilize written materials.

Allow written reports.

Develop *stop and think before speaking* strategies.

Select assignments that emphasize performance.

Have student role-play with videotape, tape recorder.

Have student read report or cue card.

Pair with peer who has good skills.

Provide peer support group.

Teach self-advocacy strategies.

Domain IX: Reading Skills/Comprehension

Characteristics

Modifications

94. Has lack of phonemic awareness (i.e., recognition that words are composed of sounds)

Teach sounds with cue word (e.g., /ĕ/ = Ed).

Provide picture cues for sounds.

Provide direct instruction.

95. Reverses letters (e.g., *b* and *d*, *saw* and *was*)

Modify delivery of instruction

- verbal,
- tape recorded,
- demonstrated, or
- diagrammatic.

96. Has difficulty reading signs in the environment

Provide model of completed work.

Utilize computer with *Arkenstone* reader.

Utilize Books on Tape.

Teach student to ask questions when confused.

Teach functional vocabulary.

Pair with peer as mentor.

Use maps marked with landmarks and/or color codes.

97. Has difficulty reading newspaper

Teach task-specific vocabulary (basic sight words, functional words).

Subscribe student to reader services for sight-impaired.

Use assistive technology (e.g., computer with *Arkenstone* reader).

98. Has difficulty reading job applications

Teach words commonly used on job applications.

Provide repeated practice with a variety of sample forms.

Provide/develop cue card (sample application) and keep available.

Help to develop a résumé.

Teach to ask for help.

Suggest completing application off-site and returning it at a later time.

(*Continues*)

99. Has difficulty reading aloud

Avoid requiring student to read aloud unless he/she has had time to practice specific passage.

100. Reading comprehension below expected level

Utilize verbal, tape-recorded, demonstrated, or diagrammatic instructions.

Provide tape-recorded manuals.

Utilize computer with *Arkenstone* reader.

Pair with peer or aide as mentor to read aloud.

Teach job-specific vocabulary.

Teach to read a paragraph and identify main ideas and facts before reading on.

Domain X: Writing/Spelling

Characteristics

Modifications

101. Has difficulty copying

Provide student with written copies of instructions, notes, etc.; do not require student to copy such material from chalkboard, overhead, or text.

Utilize assistive technology (e.g., typewriter, computer).

Utilize checklists.

102. Has difficulty writing legibly

Allow student to generate correspondence on typewriter or computer.

Allow student to use a scribe, answer orally.

Utilize assistance technology (e.g., computer with voice-input capabilities, e-mail).

103. Makes multiple spelling errors

Develop a cue card (of frequently misspelled words) and keep available.

Utilize a "misspeller's dictionary."

Develop a list of survival words.

Have mentor proofread work.

Record messages.

Utilize assistive technology (e.g., computer with spell-check capability, electronic spell check).

Grade work for value of content without points off for misspelling.

104. Has difficulty communicating through writing

Utilize correspondence samples.

Encourage use of outlines/graphic organizers.

Dictate written communications that mentor tran-scribes.

Utilize assistive technology (e.g., computer with voice-input capability).

105. Has difficulty with paragraph organization

Utilize a paragraph-writing strategy.

Encourage use of graphic organizers.

Allow student to work with a written-language tutor.

Utilize assistive technology (e.g., computer with word-processing capabilities, computer software designed to aid in the writing process).

(Continues)

106. Makes errors in grammar or punctuation

Pair with mentor to proofread work.

Dictate written communication that mentor transcribes.

Utilize assistive technology (e.g., computer with grammar-check capability).

107. Writing skills below expected level

Provide remediation to upgrade academic level.

Develop/utilize self-advocacy strategies.

Utilize assistive technology (e.g., computer with word-processing capabilities, computer with grammar- and spell-check capabilities, computer software designed to aid the writing process).

Pair with a mentor to help edit and improve written assignments.

Allow evaluation opportunities in other than written format (demonstration, oral report, projects, etc.).

Domain XI: Math

Characteristics

Modifications

108. Reverses numbers

Repeat telephone numbers and sequence to ensure accuracy.

109. Confuses math symbols

Have someone read calculations aloud to individual.

Utilize a cue card.

Teach student to underline each symbol in red before solving problem.

110. Has difficulty performing math calculations

Conduct job analysis, then develop/utilize charts, conversion tables, cue cards, flow charts, etc., of math sequences.

Utilize assistive technology (e.g., calculators, electronic measuring devices, computer software).

Have mentor proof calculations, correct missed problems.

111. Has difficulty performing math word problems

Teach problem-solving strategies.

Provide/develop diagrams, flow charts, or other visual aids.

Allow use of calculator.

112. Has difficulty managing money

Provide consumer credit counseling.

Allow use of computer software to manage finances (e.g., Quicken).

Help develop a budget based on salary and expenses.

Teach to utilize direct deposit and bank draft services.

Provide real and simulated opportunities for practice.

(Continues)

Characteristics

113. Has difficulty balancing checkbook

114. Math skills below expected level

Modifications

Pair with mentor to check calculations periodically.

Allow use of computer software (Quicken).

Allow use of calculator.

Develop/utilize task analysis checklist of sequential steps.

Provide consumer credit counseling.

Develop/provide system of natural support.

Have student participate in remediation.

Teach job-specific math skills.

Utilize assistive technology (e.g., calculator, computer).

Note. Although many individuals influenced the development of this guide, the primary authors are L. Hames, C. Dowdy, C. Nowell, and J. Carter.

APPENDIX B

Assessment Instruments

ADD-H: Comprehensive Teacher Rating Scale (ACTeRS)
Ullmann, R.K., Sleator, E.K., & Sprague, R. (1991)
MeetriTech, Inc.
111 North Market Street
Champaign, IL 61820
(800) 747–4868

ADHD Rating Scale
DuPaul, G.J. (1991)
Published in: Barkley, R.A. (1991). *Attention-Deficit
 Hyperactivity Disorder: A Clinical Workbook.* Guilford Press,
 72 Spring Street, New York, NY 10012.

Attention Deficit Disorders Evaluation Scale (ADDES)
McCarney, S.B. (1989)
Hawthorne Educational Services
800 Gray Oak Drive
Columbia, MO 65201

Attention-Deficit/Hyperactivity Disorder Test
Gilliam, J.E. (1995)
Pro-Ed
8700 Shoal Creek Boulevard
Austin, TX 78757–6897
FAX (800) FXPROED

Behavioral Assessment System for Children (BASC)
Reynolds, C.R., & Kamphaus, R.W. (1992)
American Guidance Service
Publishers Building
4201 Woodland Road
P.O. Box 99
Circle Pines, MN 55014–1796
(800) 328–2560

Child Attention Problems Rating Scale (CAP)
Edelbrock, C. (1988)
Published in: Barkley, R.A. (1991). *Attention-Deficit
    Hyperactivity Disorder: A Clinical Workbook.* Guilford Press,
    72 Spring Street, New York, NY 10012.

Comprehensive Behavior Rating Scale for Children (CBRSC)
Neeper, R., Lahey, B., & Frick, P. (1990)
Psychological Corporation
P.O. Box 839954
San Antonio, TX 78283–3954
(800) 228–0752

Conners' Teacher Rating Scales
Conners' Parent Rating Scales
Conners, C.K. (1989)
Multi-Health Systems, Inc.
North Tonawanda, NY 14120–2060

Copeland Symptom Checklist for Attention Deficit Disorders
Copeland, E.D.
Southeastern Psychological Institute
P.O. Box 12389
Atlanta, GA 30355–2389

Elementary School Situations Questionnaire
Adolescent School Situations Questionnaire
Home Situations Questionnaire
Barkley, R.A., & Edelbrock, C. (1987 version)
Published in: Barkley, R.A., & Edelbrock, C. (1987).
    Assessing situational variation in children's problem
    behaviors: The Home and School Situations
    Questionnaires. In R.J. Prinz (Ed.), *Advances in behavioral*

assessment in children and families. Greenwich, CT: JAI
  Press.
Revised version by DuPaul, G.J., & Barkley, R.A. (1992)
Published in: DuPaul, G.J., & Barkley, R.A. (1992).
  Situational variation of attention problems: Psychometric
  properties of the Revised Home and School Situations
  Questionnaires. *Journal of Clinical Child Psychology, 21*(2),
  178–188.

Goldstein Behavioral Observation Checklist
Goldstein, S., & Goldstein, M. (1985)
*The Multi-Disciplinary Evaluation and Treatment of Attention
  Disorders in Children: Symposium Handbook* (1985)
Neurology, Learning and Behavior Center
230 South 500 Street East, Suite 1100
Salt Lake City, UT 84102
(801) 532–1484

Multi-Grade Inventory for Teachers (MIT)
Arogronin, M.C., Holahan, J.M., Shaywitz, B.A., & Shaywitz,
  S.E. (1992)
Published in: *MIT* scale development, reliability, and validity
  of an instrument to assess children with attentional
  deficits and learning disabilities. In S.E. Shaywitz & B.A.
  Shaywitz (Eds.), *Attention deficit disorder comes of age.*
  Austin, TX: Pro-Ed.

Revised Behavior Problem Checklist (RBPC)
Quay, H.C., & Peterson, D.R. (1987)
Herbert Quay
University of Miami
P.O. Box 248974
Coral Gables, FL 33124
(305) 284–5208

Revised Child Behavior Checklist—Teacher Report (1991)
A Youth Self-Report (1991)
Achenbach, T., & Edelbrock, C.
Child Behavior Checklist—Parent Form (1991)
Achenbach, Thomas M.
Department of Psychiatry, University of Vermont
1 South Prospect Street
Burlington, VT 05401–3456

Social Skills Rating System (SSRS)
Gresham, F.M., & Elliott, S.N. (1990)
American Guidance Service
4201 Woodland Road
P.O. Box 99
Circle Pines, MN 55014–1796
(800) 328–2560

Teacher Observation Checklist (1988)
Social Skills Assessment (1988)
Goldstein, S.
Neurology, Learning and Behavior Center
230 South 500 Street East, Suite 1100
Salt Lake City, UT 84102

*Walker-McConnell Scale of Social Competence and School
    Adjustment*
Walker, H.M., & McConnell, S.R. (1988)
Pro-Ed
8700 Shoal Creek Boulevard
Austin, TX 78757–6897

Yale Children's Inventory (YCI)
Shaywitz, S.E., Schnell, C., Shaywitz, B.A., & Towle, V.R.
    (1986)
Published in: *Journal of Abnormal Child Psychology, 14,*
    347–354.

APPENDIX C

Resources for Professionals

Books

The ADD/Hyperactivity Handbook for Schools
Parker, H.C. (1992)
Special Needs Project
3463 State Street, #282
Santa Barbara, CA 93105
(800) 333–6867

ADHD—A Guide to Understanding and Helping Children with ADHD in School Settings
Brasswell, L. (1991)
Connecticut Association for Children with LD
18 Marshall Street
South Norwalk, CT 06854
(203) 838–5010
FAX (203) 866–6108

ADHD in the Schools: Assessment and Intervention Strategies
DuPaul, G.J., & Stoner, G. (1994)
Guilford Publications, Inc.
72 Spring Street
New York, NY 10012
(800) 365–7006

Attention Deficit Disorder—ADHD and ADD Syndromes (2nd ed.)
Jordan, D.R. (1992)
Pro-Ed
8700 Shoal Creek Boulevard
Austin, TX 78757–6897
(512) 451–3246

Attention Deficit Disorder Come of Age—Toward the Twenty-
  First Century
Shaywitz, S., & Shaywitz, B. (1992)
Pro-Ed
8700 Shoal Creek Boulevard
Austin, TX 78757–6897
(512) 451–3246

Attention Deficit Disorder: Current Understanding
Elliot, R. (1994)
18 Marshall Street
South Norwalk, CT 06854
(203) 838–5010
FAX (203) 866–6108

Attention Deficit Disorders and Hyperactivity
ERIC Clearinghouse on Disabled and Gifted Children (1996)
1920 Association Drive
Reston, VA 22091
(800) 232–7323

Attention Deficit Hyperactivity Disorder: Clinical Workbook
Barkley, R.A. (1991)
Guilford Publications, Inc.
Dept. 62
72 Spring Street
New York, NY 10012
(800) 365–7006

Attention Deficit Hyperactivity Disorder: A Handbook for
  Diagnosis and Treatment
Barkley, R.A. (1981)
Guilford Publications, Inc.
Dept. 62
72 Spring Street
New York, NY 10012
(800) 365–7006

Attention, Memory, and Executive Function
Lyon, R., & Krasnegor, N. (1996)
Paul H. Brookes Publishing
P.O. Box 10624
Baltimore, MD 21285–0624

Children with ADD: A Shared Responsibility
Council for Exceptional Children (1992)
1920 Association Drive
Reston, VA 22091
(800) 232–7323

*Educational Strategies for Students with Attention Deficit
 Disorder*
Sloane, M. (1993)
Connecticut Association for Children with LD
18 Marshall Street
South Norwalk, CT 06854
(203) 838–5010
FAX (203) 866–6108

How to Reach and Teach ADD/ADHD Children
Reif, S.F. (1993)
Center for Applied Research in Education
West Nyack, NY 10995

*Identification and Treatment of Attention Deficit Disorder: Child
 Guidance Mental Health Series*
Nussbaum, N., & Bigler, E. (1990)
Pro-Ed
8700 Shoal Creek Boulevard
Austin, TX 78757–6897
(512) 451–3246

*Managing Attention Disorders in Children: A Guide for
 Practitioners*
Goldstein, S. (1990)
Books on Special Children
P.O. Box 305
Congers, NY 10920
(914) 638–1236
FAX (914) 638–0847

Medications for Attention Disorders and Related Medical Problems
Copeland, E. (1991)
Connecticut Association for Children with LD
18 Marshall Street
South Norwalk, CT 06854
(203) 838–5010
FAX (203) 866–6108

A New Look at Attention Deficit Disorder
Nichamin, S. (1993)
Connecticut Association for Children with LD
18 Marshall Street
South Norwalk, CT 06854
(203) 838–5010
FAX (203) 866–6108

Prognosis of Attention Deficit Disorder and Its Management in Adolescence
Klein, R. Gittelman (1991)
Connecticut Association for Children with LD
18 Marshall Street
South Norwalk, CT 06854
(203) 838–5010
FAX (203) 866–6108

Section 504 and Public Schools: A Practical Guide
Streett, S., & Smith, T.E.C. (1996)
P.O. Box 251186
Little Rock, AR 72225
(501) 569–3016

Teaching Strategies: Education of Children with Attention Deficit Disorder
Chesapeake Institute
Council for Exceptional Children
1920 Association Drive
Reston, VA 22091–1589
(800) 232–7323

Games

The Stop, Relax, and Think Game
Childworks
Center for Applied Psychology, Inc.
P.O. Box 61586
King of Prussia, PA 19406
(800) 962–1141

Other Programs

Pay More Attention Self-Regulation Program
Childworks
Center for Applied Psychology, Inc.
P.O. Box 61586
King of Prussia, PA 19406
(800) 962–1141

Newsletters

The ADHD Report
Barkley, R.A., & associates
Guilford Publications, Inc.
72 Spring Street
New York, NY 10012
(800) 365–7006

Brakes: The Interactive Newsletter for Kids with ADHD
Quinn, B., & Stern, J. (1994)
Magination Press
19 Union Square West
New York, NY 10003
(800) 825–3089

Challenge
Challenge, Inc.
P.O. Box 488
West Newbury, MA 01985
(508) 462–0495

Books for Families

Parents

ADHD for Parents
Silver, L. B., M.D. (1989)
Learning Disabilities Association of America (LDA-A)
4156 Library Road
Pittsburgh, PA 15234
(412) 341–1515

ADHD/Hyperactivity: A Consumer's Guide
Connecticut Association for Children with LD (1995)
18 Marshall Street
South Norwalk, CT 06854
(203) 838–5010
FAX (203) 866–6108

Around the Clock: Parenting the ADHD Child
Goodman, J., & Hoban, S. (1994)
Guilford Publications, Inc.
72 Spring Street
New York, NY 10012
(800) 365–7006

Attention Deficit Disorder in Teenagers
Shaya, J., & Windell, J. (1995)
Learning Disabilities Association of America
4156 Library Road
Pittsburgh, PA 15234
(412) 341–1515

*Attention Deficit Disorders: Hyperactivity and Associated
   Disorders*
Coleman, W. S. (1988)
Connecticut Association for Children with LD
18 Marshall Street
South Norwalk, CT 06854
(203) 838–5010
FAX (203) 866–6108

*Attention Deficit–Hyperactivity Disorder: Is It a Learning
   Disability?*
Silver, L. (1990)
Georgetown University, School of Medicine
3800 Reservoir Road NW
Washington, DC 20007

Attention Deficit and the Macintosh
Margolies, B. (1990)
Connecticut Association for Children with LD
18 Marshall Street
South Norwalk, CT 06854
(203) 838–5010
FAX (203) 866–6108

Defiant Children: Clinician's Manual and Parent Workbook
Barkley, R.A. (1987)
Guilford Publications, Inc.
72 Spring Street
New York, NY 10012
(800) 365–7006

Fact Sheet—Attention Deficit Disorder
Council for Learning Disabilities (1995)
P.O. Box 40303
Overland Park, KS 66204
(913) 492–8755

Fact Sheet—Attention Deficit–Hyperactivity Disorder
Learning Disabilities Association of America
4156 Library Road
Pittsburgh, PA 15234
(412) 341–1515

Helping Your Child with Attention Deficit Hyperactivity Disorder
Learning Disabilities Association of America (1994)
4156 Library Road
Pittsburgh, PA 15234
(412) 341–1515

Helping Your Hyperactive Child
Taylor, J. (1990)
Connecticut Association for Children with LD
18 Marshall Street
South Norwalk, CT 06854
(203) 838–5010
FAX (203) 866–6108

How to Help Your Child with Homework (ages 6–13)
Radencich, M. C., & Schunam, J. S. (1988)
Free Spirit Publishing, Inc.
123 North Third Street, Suite 716
Minneapolis, MN 55401
(612) 338–2068

How to Own and Operate an Attention Deficit
Maxey, D. (1993)
Learning Disabilities Association of America
4156 Library Road
Pittsburgh, PA 15234
(412) 341–1515

An Introduction to Your Child Who Has Hyperkinesis
Centerwall, S. (1988)
Connecticut Association for Children with LD
18 Marshall Street
South Norwalk, CT 06854
(203) 838–5010
FAX (203) 866–6108

Management of Children and Adolescents with AD-HD (3rd Ed.)
Friedman, R., & Doyal, G. (1992)
Pro-Ed
8700 Shoal Creek Boulevard
Austin, TX 78757–6897
(512) 451–3246

*Maybe You Know My Kid: A Parent's Guide to Identifying
    ADHD*
Fowler, M.C.
Birch Lane Press
120 Enterprise Avenue
Secaucus, NJ 07094
(800) 447–2665

"Memory Skills, Study Skills," *World Book Learning Library*
Zeleny, R. O., Ed. (1986)
World Book, Inc.
Merchandise Mart Plaza
Chicago, IL 60054

Parenting Attention Deficit Disordered Teens
Landi, L. (1990)
Connecticut Association for Children with LD
18 Marshall Street
South Norwalk, CT 06854
(203) 838–5010
FAX (203) 866–6108

A Parent's Guide to Attention Deficit Disorders
Bain, L. (1991)
Childworks
Center for Applied Psychology, Inc.
P.O. Box 61586
King of Prussia, PA 19406
(800) 962–1141

Taking Charge of ADHD: The Complete Authoritative Guide for Parents
Barkley, R.
Council for Exceptional Children
1920 Association Drive
Reston, VA 22091–1589
(800) 232–7323
FAX (703) 264–1637

Children

The Don't-Give-Up Kid
Gehret, J.
Verbal Images Press
19 Fox Hill Drive
Fairport, NY 14450
(716) 377–3807

Eagle Eyes: A Child's View of Attention Deficit Disorder
Gehret, J. (1996)
Verbal Images Press
19 Fox Hill Drive
Fairport, NY 14450
(716) 377–3807

I'm Somebody Too
Gehret, J. (1995)
Verbal Images Press
19 Fox Hill Drive
Fairport, NY 14450
(716) 377–3807

Jumpin' Johnny Get Back to Work—A Child's Guide to ADHD/ Hyperactivity
Gordon, M. (1991)
Connecticut Association for Children with LD
18 Marshall Street
South Norwalk, CT 06854
(203) 838–5010
FAX (203) 866–6108

Otto Learns about His Medicine
Gaivin, M.
Childworks
Center for Applied Psychology, Inc.
P.O. Box 61586
King of Prussia, PA 19406
(800) 962–1141

Shelley, the Hyperactive Turtle
Moss, D. (1989)
Woodbine House
5615 Fishers Lane
Rockville, MD 20852
(301) 468–8800
(800) 843–7323

Sometimes I Drive My Mom Crazy, But I Know She's Crazy about Me!
Childworks (1995)
Center for Applied Psychology, Inc.
P.O. Box 61586
King of Prussia, PA 19406
(800) 962–1141

Adults with ADHD

Attention Deficit Disorder in Teenagers and Young Adults
Sloane, M. (1988)
Connecticut Association for Children with LD
18 Marshall Street
South Norwalk, CT 06854
(203) 838–5010
FAX (203) 866–6108

Hyperactive Children Grown Up (2nd Ed.)
Weiss, Gabrielle, & Hechtman, Lily Trokenberg (1993)
Guilford Publications, Inc.
72 Spring Street
New York, NY 10012
(800) 365–7006

Out of Darkness
Wolkenberg, F. (1987)
Connecticut Association for Children with LD
18 Marshall Street
South Norwalk, CT 06854
(203) 838–5010
FAX (203) 866–6108

You Mean I'm Not Lazy, Stupid, or Crazy?
Ramundo, P., & Kellys, K. (1994)
Special Needs Project
3463 State Street, #282
Santa Barbara, CA 93105
(800) 333–6867

APPENDIX E

Videotapes

A.D.D. from A to Z—A Comprehensive Guide to Attention Deficit Disorder
Bender, William, & McLaughtin, Phillip
Program 1: Characteristics of ADD
Program 2: Instructional Strategies for ADD
Program 3: Medical Interventions for ADD
Program 4: Parenting Strategies for ADD
Council for Exceptional Children
(800) 232–7323
FAX (703) 264–1637

ADHD in Adulthood: A Clinical Perspective
Robin, A.L.
Professional Advancement Seminars
1 Dix Street
Worcester, MA 01609
(508) 792–2408

ADHD in Adults
Barkley, R.A.
Guilford Publications, Inc.
72 Spring Street
New York, NY 10012
(800) 365–7006

ADHD in the Classroom: Strategies for Teachers
Barkley, R.A.
Guilford Publications, Inc.
72 Spring Street
New York, NY 10012
(800) 365–7006

ADHD: Inclusive Instruction and Collaboration Practices
Reif, Sandra (1994)
Council for Exceptional Children
1920 Association Drive
Reston, VA 22091–1589
(800) 232–7323
FAX (703) 264–1637

ADHD: What Can We Do?
Barkley, R.A.
Guilford Publications, Inc.
72 Spring Street
New York, NY 10012
(800) 365–7006

ADHD: What Do We Know?
Barkley, R.A.
Guilford Publications, Inc.
72 Spring Street
New York, NY 10012
(800) 365–7006

Attention Deficit Disorder: ADHD and ADD Syndromes
Jordan, D.R.
Pro-Ed
8700 Shoal Creek Boulevard
Austin, TX 78757–6897
(512) 451–3246

Attention Disorders: The School's Vital Role
3 C's of Childhood, Inc.
5395 Roswell Road NE, Suite 3046
Atlanta, GA 30342
(404) 986–9054

Concentration Video
Learning Disabilities Resources
P.O. Box 716
Bryn Mawr, PA 19010
(215) 525–8336
(800) 869–8336

A Continuing Education Program on ADHD
Reeve, R., Spessard, M., Walker, R., Welch, A., Wright, J., &
    Schragg, J.
Council for Exceptional Children
1920 Association Drive
Reston, VA 22091–1589
(800) 232–7323
FAX (703) 264–1637

Educating Inattentive Children: A Guide for the Classroom
Goldstein, S.
Neurology, Learning and Behavior Center
230 South 500 Street East, Suite 1100
Salt Lake City, UT 84102
(801) 532–1484

Facing the Challenges of ADD
Chesapeake Institute and the Widmeyer Group
Council for Exceptional Children
1920 Association Drive
Reston, VA 22091–1589
(800) 232–7323
FAX (703) 264–1637

Help! This Kid's Driving Me Crazy
Adkins, L., & Cady, H.
Pro-Ed
8700 Shoal Creek Boulevard
Austin, Texas 78757-6897
(512) 451–3246

It's Just Attention Disorder: A Video Guide for Kids
Goldstein, S.
Neurology, Learning and Behavior Center
230 South 500 Street East, Suite 1100
Salt Lake City, UT 84102
(801) 532–1484

Understanding Attention Deficit Disorder
Connecticut Association for Children with LD
18 Marshall Street
South Norwalk, CT 06854
(203) 838–5010

Why Won't My Child Pay Attention?
Goldstein, S.
Neurology, Learning and Behavior Center
230 South 500 Street East, Suite 1100
Salt Lake City, UT 84102
(801) 532-1484

National Associations and Support Groups

Children with Attention Deficit Disorders (CHADD)
National Headquarters
1859 North Pine Island Road, Suite 185
Plantation, FL 33322
(954) 587–3700
Local chapters available in many states

CHADD Publications
Chadder (semi-annual newsletter)
Chadder Box (monthly newsletter)
499 NW 70th Avenue, Room 308
Plantation, FL 33317

Attention Deficit Disorder Association (ADDA)
19262 Jamboree Road
Irving, CA 92715
(800) 487–2282

Learning Disabilities Association (LDA)
4156 Library Road
Pittsburgh, PA 15234
(412) 341–1515

Heath Resource Center
One Dupont Circle, #800
Washington, DC 20036
(202) 939–9320

National Information Center for Children and Youth with Handicaps (NICHY)
P.O. Box 1492
Washington, DC 20013
(800) 999–5599

National Center for Law and Learning Disabilities (NCLLD)
P.O. Box 368
Cabin John, MD 20818

References

Abikoff, H. (1991). Cognitive training in ADHD children: Less to it than meets the eye. *Journal of Learning Disabilities, 24,* 205–209.

Abikoff, H., & Gittelman, R. (1985). The normalizing effects of methylpheni-date on the classroom behavior of ADD children. *Journal of Abnormal Child Psychology, 13,* 27–38.

Abikoff, H., Gittelman, R., & Klein, D. F. (1980). Classroom observation code for hyperactive children: A replication of validity. *Journal of Consulting Clinical Psychology, 48,* 550–564.

Achenbach, T. M. (1991). *Manual for the Teachers Report Form and 1991 Profile.* Burlington, VT: University of Vermont, Department of Psychiatry.

American Psychiatric Association. (1994). Diagnostic and statistical manual of mental disorders (4th ed.). Washington, DC: Author.

Anesko, K. M., & O'Leary, S. G. (1982). The effectiveness of brief parent train-ing for the management of children's homework problems. *Child and Family Behavior Therapy, 4,* 113–127.

Anesko, K. M., Shoiock, G., Ramirez, R., & Levine, F. (1987). The homework problems checklist: Assessing children's homework difficulties. *Journal of Applied Behavioral Assessment, 9,* 179–185.

Archer, A., & Gleason, M. (1989). *Skills for school success.* North Billerica, MA: Curriculum Associates.

Archer, A., & Gleason, M. (1995). Skills for school success. In P. T. Cegelka & W. H. Berdine (Eds.), *Effective instruction for students with learning difficul-ties* (pp. 227–263). Boston: Allyn & Bacon.

Armbruster, B. B., & Anderson, T. H. (1988). On selecting "considerate" con-tent area textbooks. *Remedial and Special Education, 9,* 47–52.

Atkins, M. S., & Pelham, W. E. (1991). School-based assessment of attention deficit-hyperactivity disorder. *Journal of Learning Disabilities, 24,* 197–204.

Autry, M., Cotton, A., & Dockendorf, M. (1994). *Northside Independent School District behavior consultation model manual.* Unpublished manuscript.

Barkley, R. A. (1990). *Attention deficit hyperactivity disorder: A handbook for diag-nosis and treatment.* New York: Guilford Press.

Barkley, R. A., & Edelbrock, C. (1987). Assessing situational variation in children's problem behavior: The Home and School Situations Questionnaires. In R. J. Prinz (Ed.), *Advances in behavioral assessment of children and families.* Greenwich, CT: JAI Press.

Bauwens, J., & Hourcade, J. J. (1995). *Cooperative teaching: Rebuilding the schoolhouse for all students.* Austin, TX: PRO-ED.

Blalock, G. (1996). Community transition teams as the foundation for transition services for youth with learning disabilities. *Journal of Learning Disabilities, 29*(2), 148–159.

Blalock, G., Brito, C., Chenault, B., Detwiler, B., Hessmiller, R., Husted, D., Oney, D., Putnam, P., & Van Dyke, R. (1994). *Life span transition planning in New Mexico: A technical assistance document.* Santa Fe: New Mexico State Board of Education and State Department of Education.

Blalock, G., & Patton, J. R. (1996). Transition and students with learning disability: Creating sound futures. *Journal of Learning Disabilities, 29,* 7–16.

Bradley, C. (1937). The behavior of children receiving Benzedrine. *American Journal of Psychiatry, 94,* 571–583.

Bradley, C., & Bowen, M. (1940). School performance of children receiving amphetamine (Benzedrine) sulfate. *American Journal of Orthopsychiatry, 10,* 780–793.

Brolin, D. E. (Ed.). (1991). *Life-centered career education: A competency based approach* (3rd ed.). Reston, VA: Council for Exceptional Children.

Burcham, B., Carlson, L., & Milich, R. (1993). Promising school-based practices for students with attention deficit disorder. *Exceptional Children, 60,* 174–180.

Burcham, B. G., & DeMers, S. T. (1995). Comprehensive assessment of children and youth with ADHD. *Intervention in School and Clinic, 30*(4), 211–219.

Burnley, G. D. (1993). A team approach for identification of an attention deficit hyperactivity disorder child. *The School Counselor, 40,* 228–230.

Cantu, N. (1993). OCR clarifies evaluation requirements for ADD. *The Special Educator, 9*(1), 11–12.

Cawley, J. F., Fitzmaurice-Hayes, A. M., & Shaw, R. A. (1988). *Mathematics for the mildly handicapped: A guide to curriculum and instruction.* Boston: Allyn & Bacon.

Cawley, J. F., Goodstein, H. A., Fitzmaurice, A. M., Lepore, A., Sedlak, R., & Althaus, V. (1976). *Project MATH.* Tulsa, OK: Educational Development.

Chalmers, L. (1992). *Modifying curriculum for the special needs student in the regular classroom.* Moorhead, MN: Practical Press.

Clements, S. D., & Peters, J. E. (1962). Minimal brain dysfunction in the school-aged child. *Archives of General Psychiatry, 6,* 185–187.

Conderman, G., & Katsiyannis, A. (1995). Section 504 accommodation plans. *Intervention in School and Clinic, 31*(1), 44.

Connors, C. K. (1972). Symposium: Behavior modification of drugs: II. Psychological effects of stimulant drugs in children with minimal brain dysfunction. *Pediatrics, 49,* (702–708).

Connors, C. K., (1989). *Connors' Rating Scales.* Toronto: Multi-Health Systems.

Copeland, L., Wolraich, M., & Lindgren, S. (1987). Pediatrician's reported practices in the assessment and treatment of attention deficit disorders. *Journal of Developmental and Behavioral Pediatrics, 8*(4), 191–197.

Costello, E. J., Edelbrock, C. S., & Costello, A. J. (1985). Validity for the NIMH Diagnostic Interview schedule for children: A comparison between psychiatric and pediatric referral. *Journal of Abnormal Child Psychology, 13,* 579–595.

Council of Administrators of Special Education. (1992). *Student access: A resource guide for educators: Section 504 of the Rehabilitation Act of 1973.* Reston, VA: Author.

Council for Exceptional Children. (1992). *Children with attention deficit disorder: A shared responsibility.* Reston, VA: Author.

Cronin, M. E., & Patton, J. R. (1993). *Life skills instruction for all students with special needs: A practical guide for integrating real-life content into the curriculum.* Austin, TX: PRO-ED.

Deshler, D. D., Ellis, E. S., & Lenz, B. K. (1996). *Teaching adolescents with learning disabilities: Strategies and methods* (2nd ed.). Denver: Love Publishing.

Deshler, D. D., & Lenz, B. K. (1989). The strategies instructional approach. *International Journal of Disability, Development, and Education, 36,* 203–224.

Deshler, D. D., & Shumaker, J. B. (1986). Learning strategies: An instructional alternative for low-achieving adolescents. *Exceptional Children, 52,* 583–590.

Dougherty, E. H., & Dougherty, A. (1977). The daily report card: A simplified and flexible package for classroom behavior management. *Psychology in the Schools, 14,* 191–195.

Douglas, V. I., Barr, R. G., O'Neil, M. E., & Britton, B. G. (1986). Short-term effects of methylphenidate on the cognitive, learning, and academic performance of children with attention deficit disorder in the laboratory and classroom. *Journal of Child Psychology and Psychiatry, 27,* 191–211.

Douglas, V. I., Barr, R. G., O'Neil, M. E., & Britton, B. G. (1988). Dosage effects and individual responsibility to methylphenidate in attention deficit disorder. *Journal of Child Psychology and Psychiatry, 29,* 453–475.

Dowdy, C. A. (1996). *Strengths and Limitations Inventory: School Version.* Unpublished assessment instrument.

Duke, D. L., & Meckel, A. M. (1984). *Teacher's guide to classroom management.* New York: Random House.

Dunlap, D. K., Dunlap, G., Koegel, L. K., & Koegel, R. L. (1991). Using self-monitoring to increase independence. *Teaching Exceptional Children, 23*(3), 21.

DuPaul, G. J. (1991). Parent and teacher rating of ADHD systems: Psychometric properties in a community-based sample. *Journal of Clinical Child Psychology, 20*(3), 245–253.

Dykman, R. A., McGrew, J., & Ackerman, P. T. (1974). *A double blind clinical study of pemoline on MBD children: Comments on the psychological test results.* In C. K. Conners (Ed.), Clinical use of stimulant drugs in children. *Exerpta Medica,* 125–129.

Eisner, E. W. (1985). *The educational imagination.* New York: Macmillan.

Elksnin, L. K., & Elksnin, N. (1995). *Assessment and instruction of social skills.* San Diego: Singular.

Ellis, E. (1993). Integrative strategy instruction: A potential model for teaching content area subjects to adolescents with learning disabilities. *Journal of Learning Disabilities, 26,* 358–383.

Ellis, E., Sabornie, E., & Marshall, K. (1989). Teaching learning strategies to learning disabled students in post-secondary settings. *Academic Therapy, 24,* 491–501.

Englert, C. S., & Mariage, T. V. (1991). Shared understandings: Structuring the writing experience through dialogue. *Journal of Learning Disabilities, 24,* 330–342.

Epstein, M. H., Polloway, E. A., Foley, R., & Patton, J. R. (1993). Homework: A comparison of teachers' and parents' perceptions of the problems experienced by students identified as having behavioral disorders, learning disabilities, and no disabilities. *Remedial and Special Education, 14*(5), 40–50.

Fad, K. M. (1993). *STAND: Students taking a new direction (information packet).* Unpublished manuscript.

Fell, B., & Pierce, K. (1995). Meeting the ADD Challenge: A multi-model plan for parents, students, teachers, and physicians. *Intervention in School and Clinic, 30*(4), 198–202.

Fiore, T. A., Becker, E. A., & Nero, R. C. (1993). Educational interventions for students with attention deficit disorder. *Exceptional Children, 60,* 163–173.

Fowler, M. (1992). *CH.A.D.D. educators manual: An indepth look at attention deficit disorder from an educational perspective.* Plantation, FL: CHADD (Children with Attention Deficit Disorders).

Gadow, K. D. (1993). Attention-deficit hyperactivity disorder. In *School Dysfunction in Children and Youth*. Report of the Twenty-Fourth Ross Roundtable on Critical Pediatric Problems, pp. 52–62. Columbus, OH: Ross Products Division.

Gallagher, P. A. (1979). *Teaching students with behavior disorders: Techniques for classroom instruction*. Denver: Love Publishing.

Gardner, W. I. (1977). *Learning and behavior characteristics of exceptional children and youth*. Boston: Allyn & Bacon.

Gilliam, J. E. (1995). *Attention-deficit/hyperactivity disorder test*. Austin, TX: PRO-ED.

Goldstein, A. P., Sprafkin, R. P., Gershaw, N. J., & Klein, P. (1980). *Skillstreaming the adolescent: A structured learning approach to teaching prosocial skills*. Champaign, IL: Research Press.

Goldstein, S., & Goldstein, M. (1990). *Managing attention disorders in children: A guide for practitioners*. New York: John Wiley.

Guevremont, D. C. (1993). Social skills training: A viable treatment for ADHD? *The ADHD Report, 1*(1), 6–7.

Guevremont, D. C., DuPaul, G. J., & Barkley, R. A. (1990). Diagnosis and assessment of attention deficit hyperactivity disorder in children. *Journal of School Psychology, 28,* 51–78.

Hallahan, D. P., Lloyd, J. W., & Stoller, L. (1982). *Improving attention with self-monitoring: A manual for teachers*. Charlottesville, VA: University of Virginia.

Halloran, W. (1989). Foreword. In D. E. Berkell & J. M. Brown (Eds.), *Transition from school to work for persons with disabilities* (pp. xiii–xvi). New York: Longman.

Halpern, A. S. (1993). Quality of life as a conceptual framework for evaluating transition outcomes. *Exceptional Children, 59,* 486–498.

Halpern, A. S. (1994). The transition of youth with disabilities to adult life: A position statement of the Division on Career Development and Transition, the Council for Exceptional Children. *Career Development for Exceptional Individuals, 17,* 115–124.

Hazel, J. S., Schumaker, J. B., Sherman, J. A., & Sheldon-Wildgen, J. B. (1981). *ASSET: A social skills program for adolescents*. Champaign, IL: Research Press.

Herskowitz, J., & Rosman, N. P. (1982). *Pediatrics, neurology, and psychiatry— Common ground*. New York: Macmillan.

Holland, J. L. (1985). *Making vocational choices: A theory of vocational personalities and work environments*. Englewood Cliffs, NJ: Prentice-Hall.

Hoover, J. J., & Patton, J. R. (1995). *Teaching students with learning problems to use study skills: A teacher's guide.* Austin, TX: PRO-ED.

Hoover, J. J., & Patton, J. R. (1997). *Curriculum adaptation for students with learning and behavior problems* (2nd ed.). Austin, TX: PRO-ED.

Howe, E. M., Harris, C. W., & Tarantino, A. J. (1992). *Medical administration module.* Albany, NY: Office of Mental Retardation and Developmental Disabilities.

Idol, L., & West, J. F. (1993). Effective instruction of difficult-to-teach students: An inservice and preservice professional development program. *Intervention in School and Clinic, 29,* 47–53.

Jones, C. A., & Jones, C. R. (1995). *Comprehensive classroom management* (4th ed.). Boston: Allyn & Bacon.

Kaplan, J. S. (1990). *Beyond behavior modification: A cognitive-behavioral approach to behavior management in the school.* Austin, TX: PRO-ED.

Kelly, M. L. (1990). *Promoting children's classroom success.* New York: Guilford Press.

Kohn, A. (1993). *Punished by rewards: The trouble with gold stars, incentive plans, A's, praise, and other bribes.* Boston: Houghton Mifflin.

Kupietz, S., Winsberg, B., Richardson, E., Maitinsky, S., & Mendell, N. (1988). Effects of methylphenidate dosage on hyperactive reading-disabled children: I. Behavior and cognitive performance effects. *Journal of the American Academy of Child and Adolescent Psychiatry, 27,* 70–77.

Lambie, R. A. (1980). A systematic approach for changing materials, instruction, and assignments to meet individual needs. *Focus on Exceptional Children, 12*(1), 1–12.

Lenz, B. K., Ellis, E. S., & Scanlon, D. (1996). *Teaching learning strategies to adolescents and adults with learning disabilities.* Austin, TX: PRO-ED.

Lerner, J. W., & Lerner, S. R. (1991). Attention deficit disorder: Issues and questions. *Focus on Exceptional Children, 24,* 1–17.

Lewis, R. B., & Doorlag, D. H. (1995). *Teaching special students in the mainstream* (2nd ed.). Columbus, OH: Merrill.

Lloyd, J. W., Landrum, T., & Hallahan, D. P. (1991). Self-monitoring applications for classroom intervention. In G. Stoner, M. R. Shinn, & H. M. Walker (Eds.), *Interventions for achievement and behavior problems* (pp. 201–213). Washington, DC: National Association of School Psychologists.

Lovitt, T. C., & Horton, S. V. (1991). Adapting textbooks for mildly handicapped adolescents. In G. Stoner, M. R. Shinn, & H. M. Walker (Eds.), *Interventions for achievement and behavior problems* (pp. 439–471). Silver Springs, MD: National Association of School Psychologists.

Maker, C. J., & Nielson, A. B. (1996). *Curriculum development and teaching strategies for gifted learners* (2nd ed.). Austin, TX: PRO-ED.

Mannix, D. (1992). *Life skills activities for special children.* West Nyack, NY: The Center for Applied Research in Education.

Mannix, D. (1995). *Life skills activities for secondary students with special needs.* West Nyack, NY: The Center for Applied Research in Education.

Maryland Learning Disabilities Association. (1995). Summer Newsletter.

Mastropieri, M. A., & Scruggs, T. E. (1991). *Teaching students ways to remember: Strategies for learning mnemonically.* Cambridge, MA: Brookline Books.

Mastropieri, M. A., & Scruggs, T. E. (1993). *A practical guide for teaching science to students with special needs in inclusive settings.* Austin, TX: PRO-ED.

Mastropieri, M. A., & Scruggs, T. E. (1994). *Effective instruction for special education* (2nd ed.). Austin, TX: PRO-ED.

Mastropieri, M. A., Scruggs, T. E., Whittaker, M. E. S., & Bakken, J. P. (1994). Applications of mnemonic strategies with students with mild mental disabilities. *Remedial and Special Education, 15,* 34–43.

McBurnett, K., Lahey, B., & Pfiffner, L. (1993). Diagnosis of attention deficit disorders in DSM-IV: Scientific basis and implications for education. *Exceptional Children, 60*(2), 108–117.

McCarney, S. B. (1989). *Attention Deficit Disorder Evaluation Scale* (ADDES). Columbia, MO: Hawthorne Educational Services.

McGinnis, E., Goldstein, A. P., Sprafkin, R. P., & Gershaw, N. J. (1984). *Skillstreaming the elementary school child: A guide for teaching prosocial skills.* Champaign, IL: Research Press.

Meichenbaum, D. (1977). *Cognitive-behavior modification: An integrative approach.* New York: Plenum Press.

Montague, M., McKinney, J. D., & Hocutt, A. M. (1994). Assessing students for attention deficit disorder. *Intervention in School and Clinic, 29*(4), 212–218.

Murray, J. B. (1987). Psychophysiological effects of methylphenidate (Ritalin). *Psychological Reports, 61,* 315–336.

National Coalition of Advocates for Students. (1985). *Barriers to excellence: Our imperative for educational reform.* Washington, DC: U.S. Department of Education.

National Commission on Excellence in Education. (1983). *A nation at risk.* Washington, DC: U.S. Government Printing Office.

Nelson, J. R., Smith, D. J., Young, R. K., & Dodd, J. M. (1991). A review of self-management outcome research conducted with students with behavioral disorders. *Behavioral Disorders, 16,* 169–179.

Parker, H. G. (1988). *The ADD hyperactivity workbook for parents, teachers, and kids*. Plantation, FL: Impact Publications.

Patton, J. R. (1994). Practical recommendations for using homework with students with learning disabilities. *Journal of Learning Disabilities, 27*, 570–578.

Patton, J. R., & Dunn, C. (in press). *Transition from school to adult life for students with special needs: Basic concepts and recommended practices*. Austin, TX: PRO-ED.

Pelham, W. E., Bender, M. E., Caddel, J., Booth, S., & Moorer, S. H. (1985). Medication effect on arithmetic learning. *Archives of General Psychiatry, 42*, 948–951.

Pfiffner, L., & Barkley, R. (1990). Educational placement and classroom management. In R. Barkley (Ed.), *Attention deficit hyperactivity disorder: A handbook for diagnosis and treatment* (pp. 498–539). New York: Guilford Press.

Physician's Desk Reference. (1994). Oravell, NJ: Medical Economics Company.

Polloway, E. A., Bursuck, W. D., Jayanthi, M., Epstein, M. H., & Nelson, J. S. (1996). Treatment acceptability: Determining appropriate interventions within inclusive classrooms. *Intervention in School and Clinic, 31*, 133–144.

Polloway, E. A., Epstein, M. H., Bursuck, W., Jayanthi, M., & Cumblad, C. (1994). A national survey of classroom practices concerning homework. *Journal of Learning Disabilities, 27*, 500–509.

Polloway, E. A., & Patton, J. R. (1993). *Strategies for teaching learners with special needs* (5th ed.). Columbus, OH: Merrill/Macmillan.

Polloway, E. A., & Patton, J. R. (1997). *Strategies for teaching learners with special needs* (6th ed.). Columbus, OH: Merrill/Prentice-Hall.

Polloway, E. A., Patton, J. R., Payne, J. S., & Payne, R. A. (1989). *Strategies for teaching learners with special needs* (4th ed.). Columbus, OH: Merrill.

Prater, M. A., Joy, R., Chilman, B., Temple, J., & Miller, S. R. (1991). Self-monitoring of on-task behavior by adolescents with learning disabilities. *Learning Disability Quarterly, 14*, 164–177.

Puig-Antich, J., & Chambers, W. (1978). *The schedule for affective disorder and schizophrenia for school-aged children*. New York: New York Psychiatric Institute.

Quay, H. C., & Peterson, D. R. (1983). *Interim marval for the revised Behavior Problem Checklist*. Coral Gables, FL: Author.

Reeve, R. E. (1990). ADHD: Facts and fallacies. *Intervention in School and Clinic, 26*, 71–78.

Reid, R., Maag, J. W., & Vasa, S. F. (1994). Attention deficit hyperactivity disorder as a disability category: A critique. *Exceptional Children, 60*, 198–214.

Reid, R. C., Allard, K. E., & Hofmeister, A. M. (1993). The SECTOR courseware evaluation form. In J. D. Lindsey (Ed.), *Computers and exceptional individuals* (2nd ed., pp. 389–398). Austin, TX: PRO-ED.

Reisberg, L. (1990). Curriculum evaluation and modification: An effective teaching perspective. *Intervention in School and Clinic, 26,* 99–105.

Riccio, C. A., Hynd, G. W., Cohen, M., & Gonzalez, J. J. (1993). Neurological basis of attention deficit hyperactivity disorder. *Exceptional Children, 60,* 118–124.

Richardson, E., Kupietz, S., & Maitinsky, S. (1987). What is the role of academic intervention in the treatment of hyperactive children with reading disorders? In J. Loney (Ed.), *The young hyperactive child: Answers to questions about diagnosis, prognosis, and treatment.* New York: Haworth Press.

Richardson, E., Kupietz, S. S., Winsberg, B. G., Maitinsky, S., & Mendell, N. (1988). Effects of methylphenidate dosage in hyperactive reading disabled children: II. Reading achievement. *Journal of the American Academy of Child and Adolescent Psychiatry, 27,* 78–87.

Rief, S. F. (1993). *How to reach and teach ADD/ADHD children.* Boston: Allyn & Bacon.

Roderique, T. W., Polloway, E. A., Cumblad, C., Epstein, M. H., & Bursuck, W. (1994). Homework: A survey of policies in the United States. *Journal of Learning Disabilities, 27,* 481–487.

Rooney, K. (1988). *Independent strategies for efficient study.* Richmond, VA: J. R. Enterprises.

Rooney, K. (1989). Independent strategies for efficient study: A core approach. *Academic Therapy, 24,* 389–390.

Rooney, K. (1993). *Attention deficit hyperactivity disorder: A videotape program.* Richmond, VA: State Department of Education.

Rooney, K. J. (1995). Dyslexia revisited: History, educational philosophy, and clinical assessment applications. *Intervention in School and Clinic, 31*(1), 6–15.

Rooney, K., Hallahan, D. P., & Lloyd, J. W. (1984). Self-recording of attention by learning disabled students in the regular classroom. *Journal of Learning Disabilities, 17,* 360–364.

Runge, A., Walker, J., & Shea, T. (1975). A passport to positive parent-teacher communications. *Teaching Exceptional Children, 7*(3), 91–92.

Safer, D. J., & Krager, J. M. (1988). A survey of medication treatment for hyperactive/inattentive students. *Journal of the American Medical Association, 260,* 2256–2258.

Sargent, L. R. (1991). *Social skills for school and community: Systematic instruction for children and youth with cognitive delays.* Reston, VA: Division on Mental Retardation and Developmental Disabilities, Council for Exceptional Children.

Schachar, R., Sandberg, S., & Rutter, M. (1986). Agreement between teacher ratings and observations of hyperactivity, inattentiveness, and defiance. *Journal of Abnormal Child Psychology, 14,* 331–335.

Schaughency, E. A., & Rothlind, J. (1991). Assessment and classification of attention deficit hyperactive disorders. *School Psychology Review, 20,* 197–202.

Schloss, P. J., Smith, M. A., & Schloss, C. N. (1995). *Instructional methods for adolescents with learning and behavior problems* (2nd ed.). Boston: Allyn & Bacon.

Schumaker, J. B., Deshler, D. D., Alley, G. R., & Denton, D. H. (1982). Multipass: A learning strategy for improving comprehension. *Learning Disability Quarterly, 5,* 295–304.

Schumaker, J. B., Deshler, D. D., Nolan, S., Clark, F. L., Alley, G. R., & Warren, M. M. (1981). *Error monitoring strategy: A learning strategy for improving academic performance of LD adolescents.* (Research Report No. 32). Lawrence: University of Kansas Institute for Research on Learning Disabilities.

Schumm, J. S., & Strickler, K. (1991). Guidelines for adapting content area textbooks: Keeping teachers and students content. *Intervention in School and Clinic, 27,* 79–84.

Scott, P., & Raborn, D. T. (1995). *Realizing the gift of diversity among students with learning disabilities.* Albuquerque, NM: University of New Mexico.

Scruggs, T. E., & Mastropieri, M. A. (1989). Reconstructive elaborations: A model for content area learning. *American Educational Research Journal, 26,* 311–327.

Scruggs, T. E., & Mastropieri, M. A. (1992). *Teaching test-taking skills: Helping students show what they know.* Cambridge, MA: Brookline Books.

Scruggs, T. E., & Mastropieri, M. A. (1994). Successful mainstreaming in elementary science classes: A qualitative study of three reputational cases. *American Educational Research Journal, 31,* 785–811.

Serna, L., & Patton, J. R. (1997). Effective teaching practices. In E. A. Polloway & J. R. Patton (Eds.), *Strategies for teaching learners with special needs* (6th ed., pp. 135–173). Columbus, OH: Merrill/Prentice-Hall.

Shannon, T., & Polloway, E. A. (1993). Promoting error monitoring in middle school students with learning disabilities. *Intervention in School and Clinic, 28,* 160–164.

Shaywitz, S. E., Schnell, C., Shaywitz, B. A., & Towle, V. R. (1986). Yale Children's Inventory (YSI): An instrument to assess children with attention deficits and learning disabilities: Scale development and psychometric properties. *Journal of Abnormal Child Psychology, 14,* 347–364.

Silbert, J., Carnine, D., & Stein, M. (1990). *Direct instruction mathematics* (2nd ed.). Columbus, OH: Merrill/Prentice-Hall.

Smith, P. B., & Bentley, G. (1975). *Facilitator manual, teacher training program: Mainstreaming mildly handicapped students in the regular classroom.* Austin, TX: Education Service Center, Region XII.

Smith, T. E. C., Finn, D. F., & Dowdy, C. A. (1993). *Teaching students with mild disabilities.* Fort Worth: Harcourt & Brace.

Smith, T. E. C., Polloway, E. A., Patton, J. R., & Dowdy, C. A. (1995). *Teaching students with special needs in inclusive settings.* Boston: Allyn & Bacon.

Stephens, K. R. (1996). Product development for gifted students. *Gifted Child Today Magazine, 19*(6), 18–20.

Strauss, A. S., & Lehtinen, L. E. (1947). *Psychopathology and education in brain-injured children.* New York: Grune & Stratton.

Strichart, S. S., & Mangrum, C. T. (1993). *Teaching study strategies to students with learning disabilities.* Boston: Allyn & Bacon.

Strother, D. B. (1984). Too much, just right, or not enough? *Phi Delta Kappan, 28,* 423–426.

Super, D. (1995). *Life roles, values, and career., International findings of the work importance study* (1st ed.). The Jossey-Bass Social and Behavioral Science Series. ED389914.

Swanson, J. M., McBurnett, K., Wigal, T., Pfiffner, L. J., Lerner, M. A., Williams, L., Christian, D. L., Tamm, L., Willcutt, E., Crowley, K., Clevenger, W., Khouzam, N., Woo, C., Crinella, F. M., & Fisher, T. D. (1993). Effect of stimulant medication on children with attention deficit disorder: A "review of reviews." *Exceptional Children, 60,* 154–162.

Turnbull, A. P., & Turnbull, H. R. (1986). *Families, professionals, and exceptionality: A special partnership.* New York: Merrill.

Turvey, J. S. (1986). Homework: Its importance to student achievement. *NASSP Bulletin, 70*(487), 27–35.

Ullmann, R. K., & Sleator, E. K. (1985). Attention deficit disorder children with and without hyperactivity: Which behaviors are helped by stimulants? *Clinical Pediatrics, 24,* 547–551.

Ullman, R. K., Sleator, E. K., & Sprague, R. (1984). A new rating scale for diagnosis and monitoring of ADD children. *Psychopharmacology Bulletin, 70,* 160–165.

U.S. Department of Education (1990). *National Assessment of Educational Progress Report.* Washington, DC: Author.

Vocational Rehabilitation Act Amendments of 1973, 29 U.S.C. §701 *et seq.*

Walker, H. M., McConnell, S., Holmes, D., Todis, B., Walker, J., & Golden, N. (1983). *The Walker social skills curriculum: The ACCEPTS program.* Austin, TX: PRO-ED.

Walker, J. E., & Shea, T. M. (1988). *Behavior management: A practical approach for educators* (4th ed.). New York: Merrill/Macmillan.

Wallander, J. L., Schroeder, S. R., Michelli, J. A., & Gualitieri, C. T. (1987). Classroom social interaction of attention deficit disorder with hyperactivity children as a function of stimulant medication. *Journal of Pediatric Psychology, 12,* 61–76.

Wehman, P. (1995). *Individual Transition Plans: The Teacher's Curriculum Guide for Helping Youth with Special Needs.* Austin, TX: PRO-ED.

Weiner, R., Reich, W., Herjanic, B., Jung, K. G., & Amado, H. (1987). Reliability, validity, and parent-child agreement studies of the Diagnostic Interview for Children and Adolescents (DICA). *Journal of the American Academy of Child and Adolescent Psychiatry, 26,* 649–653.

Werner, H., & Strauss, A. S. (1941). Pathology of the figure-background relation in the child. *Journal of Abnormal & Social Psychology, 36,* 234–248.

West, J. F., Idol, L., & Cannon, G. (1989). *Collaboration in the schools.* Austin, TX: PRO-ED.

Westling, D. L., & Koorland, M. A. (1988). *The special educator's handbook.* Boston: Allyn & Bacon.

Whalen, C. K., Henker, B., Swanson, J. M., Granger, D., Kliewer, W., & Spencer, J. (1987). Natural social behaviors in hyperactive children: Dose effects of methylphenidate. *Journal of Consulting and Clinical Psychology, 55,* 187–193.

Winton, P. (1986). Effective strategies for involving families in intervention efforts. *Focus on Exceptional Children, 19*(2), 1–10.

Wodrich, D. L. (1994). *What every parent wants to know: Attention deficit hyperactivity disorder.* Baltimore: Brookes Publishing.

Wood, J. W. (1984). *Adapting instruction for the mainstream.* Columbus, OH: Charles Merrill.

Workman, E. A., & Katz, A. M. (1995). *Teaching behavioral self-control to students* (2nd ed.). Austin, TX: PRO-ED.

Worthington, L. A., Patterson, D., Elliott, E., & Linkous, L. (1993). *Assessment of children with ADHD: An inservice education program for educator and parents.* Unpublished manuscript. University of Alabama, Department of Special Education, Tuscaloosa.

Zentall, S. S. (1993). Research on the educational implications of attention deficit hyperactivity disorder. *Exceptional Children, 60,* 143–153.

Index

Notes

Notes

_____

_____

_____

_____

_____

_____

_____

_____

_____

_____

_____

_____

_____

_____

_____

_____

_____

_____

_____

_____

_____

_____

_____

Notes

Notes

Notes